Complete CAE

Workbook *without answers*

Laura Matthews and Barbara Thomas

CAMBRIDGE
UNIVERSITY PRESS

CAMBRIDGE UNIVERSITY PRESS
Cambridge, New York, Melbourne, Madrid, Cape Town, Singapore,
São Paulo, Delhi, Dubai, Tokyo

Cambridge University Press
The Edinburgh Building, Cambridge CB2 8RU, UK

www.cambridge.org
Information on this title: www.cambridge.org/9780521698481

© Cambridge University Press 2009

First published 2009
Reprinted 2010

Printed in the United Kingdom at the University Press, Cambridge

A catalogue record for this publication is available from the British Library

ISBN 978-0-521-69843-6 Student's Book with answers with CD-ROM
ISBN 978-0-521-69842-9 Student's Book without answers with CD-ROM
ISBN 978-0-521-69845-0 Teacher's Book
ISBN 978-0-521-69847-4 Class Audio CDs (3)
ISBN 978-0-521-69844-3 Student's Book Pack
ISBN 978-0-521-69849-8 Workbook with answers with Audio CD
ISBN 978-0-521-69848-1 Workbook without answers with Audio CD

Contents

Unit title	Reading	Writing	Use of English
1 Our people	Reading Part 3: A visit home		
2 Mastering languages		A report	• Use of English Part 4 • Use of English Part 5
3 All in the mind	Reading Part 1: The cocktail party effect, What is intelligence?, What's in a face?	CAE writing tasks	
4 Office space		Functional phrases	• Use of English Part 3: Putting some fun into the workplace • Use of English Part 5
5 Dramatic events	Reading Part 2: The scariest ride on the planet		
6 Picture yourself		Correcting your writing	• Use of English Part 1: The Kogod courtyard • Use of English Part 3: Performance art
7 Leisure and entertainment	Reading Part 4: World music reviews: artists and albums	A proposal	
8 Don't blame the media		Giving a positive or negative impression	• Use of English Part 2: Effects of television on childhood literacy • Use of English Part 5
9 At top speed	Reading Part 3: John Paul Stapp: The fastest man on earth	Punctuation	
10 A lifelong process		Ways of linking ideas	• Use of English Part 4 • Use of English Part 2: Electronic voting system
11 Being somewhere else	Reading Part 4: Travel writing	Correcting your writing	
12 The living world		Correcting your spelling	• Use of English Part 4 • Use of English Part 1: The beauty of the beasts
13 Health and lifestyle	Reading Part 1: Mike Powell, award-winning photojournalist, Coaching athletes for competitions, Extract from a novel: a game of squash	Formal writing	
14 Moving abroad		Checking your writing	• Use of English Part 2: Ellis Island • Use of English Part 3: Advice to families moving abroad

Listening	Vocabulary	Grammar
Listening Part 4: People talking about a friend	Collocations with *give*, *do* and *make*	• Verb forms to talk about the past • *Used to* • *Used to* and *be/get used to*
Listening Part 3: An Irish-Australian writer and broadcaster discusses the Irish-Gaelic language	• Phrasal verbs with *get* • Word building	Expressing purpose, reason and result
Listening Part 1: An incident involving a lorry, an interview with a zoo director, a conversation about a stonemason	Word building	The passive
Listening Part 4: People talking about their jobs	• Adjective/noun collocations • *work* and *job* • Formation of adverbs	Expressing possibility, probability and certainty
Listening Part 3: An interview with a woman who was rescued from a sinking yacht	• Compound nouns • Phrasal verbs with *take*	Infinitives and verb + *-ing* forms
Listening Part 1: Two friends talking about a book, two people talking about a piece of jewellery, two sisters talking about clothes for a special occasion	• Adjective/noun collocations • Synonyms	Avoiding repetition
Listening Part 2: A professional dancer talking to a group of young people about dancing as a career	The verb *to pay*	Ways of linking ideas
Listening Part 4: People talking about their jobs in television	Television, newspapers and computers	Reported speech
Listening Part 2: A talk about an adventure race	Word building	Tenses in time clauses and time adverbials
Listening Part 1: Two people talking about studying abroad, two people talking in a shop, an interview with a trapeze artist	• Expressions with prepositions: *at*, *in* and *on* • Word building	Expressing ability, possibility and obligation
Listening Part 3: A writer talking about the Brooklyn Bridge in New York	Phrasal verbs: word order with pronouns	• Conditionals • *At*, *in* and *on* to express location
Listening Part 1: A radio discussion about Monarch butterflies, two friends talking about a cookery competition, two friends discussing a trip to a game park	Word building	• Uncountable nouns • Verbs followed by prepositions • Articles
Listening Part 2: A talk about the history of surfing	Word building	The language of comparison
Listening Part 2: A man talking to a group of people about living in Romania	Phrasal verbs with *give*, *do* and *make*	• Emphasis: cleft sentences • Comment adverbials

Unit 1 Our people

Grammar
Verb forms to talk about the past

❶ **Read part of a story about a woman returning home and then put the verbs in brackets into the correct past tense.**

As Anne drove west, she **(1)** ....*felt*........ (feel) almost as though she were driving in a dream. But as she **(2)** .... (get) closer to home, there was an excitement she **(3)** .... (not experience) for years. She **(4)** .... (live) abroad for so long that she **(5)** .... (forget) what it was like to feel that you really belonged somewhere. Her family were there, in her village, and they **(6)** .... (wait) for her. As she **(7)** .... (come) over the hill, the view **(8)** .... (be) the same as it **(9)** .... (always / be). She noticed a young man who **(10)** .... (walk) purposefully towards the centre of the village. As the car drew near, he **(11)** .... (turn) and **(12)** .... (nod) as people do in this part of the world. She **(13)** .... (not realise) until then that it was Niall, a boy she **(14)** .... (babysit) many times when she was a teenager. So not everything **(15)** .... (stay) the same. Anne herself **(16)** .... (also / change) of course. The night before, she **(17)** .... (stay) in a hotel in Dublin and the receptionist **(18)** .... (ask) her '**(19)** .... (you / be) to Ireland before?' But what could she expect when her accent **(20)** .... (almost / disappear)?

❷ **Read each pair of sentences and then answer the question which follows.**

1 **A** Katrina studied Portuguese when she arrived in Brazil.
  B Katrina has been studying Portuguese since she arrived in Brazil.

In which sentence is Katrina still in Brazil? .....*B*.....

2 **A** My brother was always borrowing my things when we were teenagers.
  B My brother always borrowed my things when we were teenagers.

In which sentence does the speaker seem slightly irritated? ....

3 **A** Has Richard rung this morning?
  B Did Richard ring this morning?

In which sentence is it still morning? ....

4 **A** My school team won the regional championship five times.
  B My school team has won the regional championship five times since 1997.

In which sentence does the speaker think the team might win the regional championship again? ....

5 **A** When Giulia got home, her friends made her a meal.
  B When Giulia got home, her friends had made her a meal.

In which sentence was the meal ready when Giulia arrived? ....

Used to

❸ Look at the past tense verbs in these sentences. Rewrite any sentence where the verb can be replaced by *used to*. Write 'No' for any sentence that cannot be changed.

Did parents use to be

1 ~~Were parents~~ stricter with their children fifty years ago, do you think?

2 After I left school, I went abroad twice to work as an au pair.

3 People wrote letters by hand or on a typewriter until computers became widespread.

4 Is lunch still as important in your country as it was?

5 My father has worked in different countries so I've been to lots of different schools.

6 I spent last summer helping my grandparents decorate their house.

7 Did you get as stressed at your last job as you do here?

8 I speak Russian quite well as I studied it for four years.

9 Japanese people didn't eat as much chicken or pork in the past as they do now.

10 Wasn't there a factory on this site until a few years ago?

Used to and be/get used to

❹ ⊙ *Used to* and *be/get used to* have different meanings and forms. Look at these sentences written by CAE students. Find the mistake in each one and then correct it.

used

1 The children hate walking because they are ~~use~~ to going everywhere by car.

2 Some students are used to eat a snack during classes.

3 Hockey didn't used to be very popular in Spain.

4 Even if you find joining a new school difficult at first, you will soon get used to.

5 Were you used to work under pressure in your old job?

6 If you do not used to walking every day, you will find a trekking holiday very difficult.

7 Have you got used to cook for yourself?

8 Jose use to be a good swimmer when he was younger.

9 Travel helps you be used to different ways of doing things.

10 Laura was used to have a lot of noise around her because she came from a big family.

Vocabulary
Collocations with *give, do* and *make*

⊙ Look at these sentences written by CAE students and then choose the correct verb.

1 Our college (*gives*)/ *makes* us a wide choice of subjects to study.

2 The students were asked to *give*/*make* their opinions about the new menu in the canteen.

3 We *do/make* a lot of business with American companies.

4 I would like your newspaper to *do/make* me an apology.

5 I have *done/made* hundreds of exercises on grammar and vocabulary this week.

6 We can *give/make* a discount to our regular customers.

7 The strike didn't *do/make* any harm to local businesses.

8 Silva *gave/made* a remark about her sister which I thought was a bit unkind.

9 The college hopes to *do/make* a profit by selling its magazine.

10 The bus company has *done/made* improvements to the services it offers.

11 It is too late to repair some of the damage *done/made* to the environment.

12 It is worth *doing/making* an effort to look back at what you've learnt.

13 Nowadays both men and women *do/make* the housework but it wasn't like that in the past.

14 You will have to *do/make* your own bed every morning while you are living here.

15 The band *gave / made* the best performance of their lives last night.

You are going to read an extract from an autobiography. For questions 1–7, choose the answer (A, B, C or D) which you think fits best according to the text.

A Visit Home

Amid the swarming, clattering travellers, railway staff and suitcases, I saw the thick, dark eyebrows of my brother Guy lift by approximately one millimetre in greeting as I came down the steps of the footbridge and out into the station forecourt. Guy speaks like most men in the village we come from, i.e. not at all until he has spent five minutes considering whether there are other means of communication he can use instead. His favourites are the eyebrow-raise, the shrug, and the brief tilt of his chin;
line 10 if he is feeling particularly emotional, he may perform all three together. That morning, as I worked my bags through the other passengers, he kept his eyebrows raised. Standing in his work clothes, he looked rather out of place, resembling a large, solitary rusty nail in the midst of, but apart from, the crowd of people: his steel-capped boots, battered, formless jacket and heavy stubble seemed to be causing many people to give him
line 18 a wide berth, diverting their path to the exit rather than heading for it directly.

'Hello, Guy,' I said.

'Now then,' he replied. 'Give me one of your bags.'

'Thank you,' I said, and passed him a large bag.

'Whatever have you got in here?' he exclaimed.

My brother is appalled by indulgences such as luggage, although his exclamations are less aggressive than resignedly bemused. With Guy, you have to understand that when he asks what on earth you've got in a bag, it is a way of saying, 'Hello, how are you?'

'It'll be the computer that's heavy. And there are some books,' I explained.

'Books,' he said wearily, shaking his head.

'Sorry.'

'Doesn't matter,' he said. 'It's not that heavy.' He yanked the bag up onto his shoulder.

'It's nice to see you, Guy.'

Guy raised his eyebrows and chin five millimetres, and strode off towards the car park.

I felt relieved by his distracted, unemotional expression because it was usual: since he was a small child he had gone through much of life looking as if he was pondering the answer to a complex mathematical problem. But as I caught up with him and looked at him from the side, I noticed dark half-circles below his eyes.

'Are you all right, then?' I said.

He raised his eyebrows again, and blew out through pursed lips. He looked as if he were trying to pop the features off his face. Then he gave me the sort of consolation smile you give people when they've asked a stupid question, batted his lashy black-brown eyes and shrugged.

'You look a bit worn out,' I said.

'I should think I do,' he said. 'I've been doing twelve-hour days on the farm since July. Sling your bags into the back of the van then.'

This was not as straightforward as he made it sound. He used the van as a workshop, storage unit and mobile home, and so as well as the usual driving-dregs of sweet wrappers and plastic bottles, there was farm equipment of an often surprising scale – straw bales, black polythene barrels, bundles of shovels and forks, metal toolboxes which were themselves almost as large as small cars, and other tools which I did not recognise or understand. Intermingled with that were random, inexplicable household articles: sofa cushions, half a dozen plant pots and a roll of carpet.

I gingerly balanced my bags on some boxes, and then walked round the van and climbed into the front passenger seat. Guy stamped down the accelerator and we shot out of the car park. Guy looked straight ahead into the traffic, lifted his eyebrows and moved his mouth in what may or may not have been a grin. As we drove through the city, I watched his face to try to catch his expression when the half-grin lapsed, but he just lost himself in nonchalant concentration on the other cars and vans around us. For something to do, I turned on the radio and began retuning it. This caused a very loud static noise to fill the cab, and Guy to jerk round in his seat, shouting, 'Don't fiddle with that radio.'

I snapped it off, and looked at him again. 'Sorry.'

'Never mind,' he said. 'It only plays one station and it

takes me ages to get that. There are some CDs in the glove compartment. Put one of those on instead.'

I put a CD on but as we accelerated off at the bypass roundabout the music was drowned out by the engine noise anyway.

It takes only twenty minutes to drive through the hills to our village, but that day the journey seemed to take forever. Neither of us could think of anything to say to each other so Guy pretended to concentrate on the speed of his windscreen wipers which were keeping the driving rain off the windscreen so he could see the road ahead. I, on the other hand, leant my forehead against the side window, looking out at the scenery which was so familiar to me but was actually obliterated by the horizontal rain.

Richard Benson, author of extract 'A visit home', signing copies of his book The Farm.

1 What aspect of Guy's personality is the writer reinforcing when he says 'if he is feeling particularly emotional, he may perform all three together' (lines 10–11)?

A His facial expressions are difficult to interpret.

B His speech is always backed up by non-verbal expressions.

C He is very controlled when expressing his feelings.

D He can give out conflicting messages about what he is thinking.

2 What is meant by many people giving Guy 'a wide berth' (line 18)?

A People were staring at him because of the way he looked.

B People were getting annoyed with him because he was in their way.

C People did not understand what he was doing there.

D People did not feel comfortable getting too close to him.

3 How does the writer feel when Guy complains about his bag?

A He knows he shouldn't take the complaint seriously.

B He thinks Guy is making an unnecessary fuss.

C He wishes Guy had not greeted him with a complaint.

D He is embarrassed about bringing so much luggage.

4 As they walk towards the car park, the writer realises that

A he is not being sensitive enough about Guy's situation.

B there is a change in Guy's normal behaviour.

C Guy's expression seems more worried than usual.

D he had more reason to be concerned about Guy than he initially thought.

5 What does the writer exaggerate when he is describing the back of the van?

A the combination of items

B the size of some of the contents

C how old some of the contents were

D how many items were unnecessary

6 Guy gets annoyed in the van because

A the radio doesn't work properly.

B he prefers to listen to CDs.

C the radio made a terrible noise.

D his brother touched the radio.

7 What does the writer say about the journey in the van?

A He preferred to look out at the countryside rather than talk.

B He didn't speak to Guy because the driving conditions were difficult.

C The fact that they travelled in silence seemed to make it longer.

D It was much slower than usual because of the weather.

Listening Part 4

You will hear five short extracts in which people are talking about their friends.

TASK ONE

For questions **1–5**, choose from the list (**A–H**) how each speaker originally met their friend.

TASK TWO

For questions **6–10**, choose from the list (**A–H**) the quality each speaker's friend has.

While you listen you must complete both tasks.

A at a musical event	Speaker 1	1
B on public transport		
C through a relative	Speaker 2	2
D at school		
E through another friend	Speaker 3	3
F at work		
G at a sporting event	Speaker 4	4
H as a neighbour	Speaker 5	5

A a talent for listening	Speaker 1	6
B a reluctance to criticise		
C a desire to share	Speaker 2	7
D willingness to apologise		
E kindness to others	Speaker 3	8
F enthusiasm for new ideas		
G an ability to keep secrets	Speaker 4	9
H continual optimism	Speaker 5	10

Unit 2 Mastering languages

Grammar

Expressing purpose, reason and result

❶ ⓐ Read this extract from a principal's letter and then complete the gaps with one of the phrases from the box below.

> with the result that   led to   ~~so as to~~
> with the intention of   due to

Allerton Moor
High School

Dear parent,

As you know, we have recently reduced the length of the school day and cut the length of breaks between lessons **(1)** ....*so as to*.......... maintain an orderly and purposeful movement of pupils around the premises.

I am pleased to report that, **(2)** ....*due to*........... the pupils very positive response to the idea, the transition to the new timetable has been accomplished, with the minimum of disruption. It has, in addition, **(3)** ....*led to*............ increased concentration levels, **(4)** *with the result tha* most staff report a better learning environment.

I would also like to emphasise that we introduced this shorter school day **(5)** *with the intention of* offering a much wider choice of extra-curricula activities, including sport and music. I am therefore delighted to report record enrolments for these activities.

Yours faithfully,

Dr Tim Mortimer
Principal.

ⓑ Read part of a dialogue between two friends and then complete the gaps with one of the phrases from the box below.

> make sure that   means   ~~otherwise~~   in case   so

Well, I'd better go now, Anna, **(1)** ....*otherwise*.......... I'll be late for my music lesson. Shall I call you later **(2)** ....*so*................ we can talk about where to meet up tomorrow?

Yeah, do that. The drama workshop in London starts at about 10.00am, which **(3)** ....*means*......... an early start. We should **(4)** *make sure that* we know the times of trains, **(5)** ....*in case*...... we don't have much time to spare when we reach the station.

Vocabulary
Phrasal verbs with *get*

1 ⓐ Match the two halves of the sentence.

1 I'd like you to just sit tight
2 How can they get away with
3 We've accepted the invitation for the party,
4 I know you don't want to write your essay
5 I've had flu for three weeks
6 Once you've got into a difficult situation,
7 A teenage hacker managed to
8 I woke up when it got light at 4.00am
9 I decided not to get into an argument
10 My neighbour is very friendly,
11 I hate going to the dentist,
12 I've always got on well with my brother,

a it's very hard to get out!
b with my parents about staying out late.
c get into the phone company records.
d so I'll just have to get it over with.
e but I think you should just get on with it.
f and didn't get back to sleep again.
g but I know that nobody else does.
h charging £20 for a meal like that?
i but it's hard to get away if she's talking.
j until I get home in an hour or so.
k and it's great to get back to normal.
l so we can't get out of going to it now.

ⓑ Complete these sentences in your own words.

a I often try to get out of ....
b I'd never get into an argument about.. .
c I try to get out of difficult situations by ....
d I usually get on well with ....

Word building

2 ⓐ Write each of the suffixes from the box below into the appropriate circle.

| -able -(u)al -ally -(e)n -ful -hood -ical -ify |
| -ise -ity -less -ly -ment -ness -ship |

ⓑ Now make words for each circle using the base words in the box below.

| broad class disappoint false fantasy |
| habit hard harm maximum nation purpose |
| reason scarce special taste thick wide |

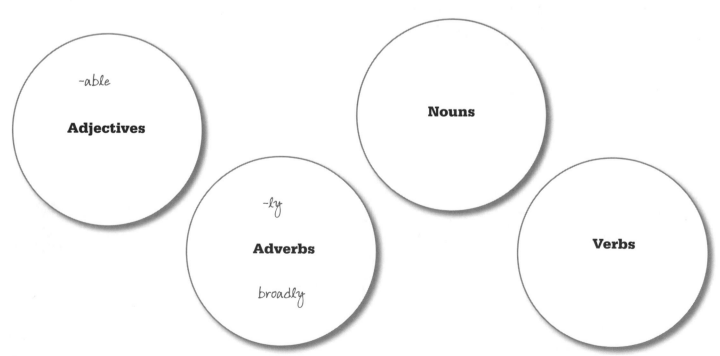

Writing

A report

⊙ **Read the paragraphs, A–E below, written by a CAE student, and then put them into the correct order, using the linking phrases to help you. Then read each paragraph again and correct the spelling mistakes (there are 15 in total).**

The correct order is: **1** .... **2** .... **3** .... **4** .... **5** ....

REPORT ON OUR ENGLISH LANGUAGE COURSE

A I also appreciated the fact that the accomodation was in host families – it is a very good idea as more opportunity for practising language is given. Unfortunetely, however, I lived some distance from the school and there were some unforeseen problems with the local transport. And one other comment I'd like to make is that what also needs improvement is the school cantean. The food was almost inedible, and there was remarkably little choice.

B On the whole, however, I must admit the course helped me develop my language skills and I lernt a lot of new language. I think, therefore, that in spite of some inconveniance such as transport or food problems, the course deserves recomendation for other trainees.

C In general, the course was well organized and the objectives fulfilled. What I appreciated most was the oportunity to improve my speaking skills. The teachers were very frendly and encouraged us to use the language and, as a result, the course gave me confidance. However, although I was pleased with my progress, in my opinion there could have been some more writting classes, as all of us needed these skills for our future use.

D Following your request I am submiting a report on the English course I attended in April this year. The aim of the course was to teach the participents English vocabulary as well as to develop and improve all our language skills.

E In addition, I think that the publisity about individual study was misleading. The study centre was poorly equipped, and the language laboratory frequently broke down, so you could hardly rely on them as aids for developing your listening skills. But what I did benefit from was a computer room with programes reinforcing the knowledge acquired during classes.

Use of English Part 4

For questions 1–5, think of one word only which can be used appropriately in all three sentences. Here is an example (0).

0 Educational reforms will be at the ....*top*......... of the government's agenda next week.
As he left for work, Peter gave his young daughter a quick kiss on the ....*top*......... of her head.
At 4.00 am, the climbers could just see the sun rising over the ....*top*......... of the mountain to the east.

1 I know that Peter is .... articulate, so I can understand why he likes public speaking.
All the film reviews I read of *Star Waves* recommended it very .... indeed.
Paula Strang's new novel must be one of the most .... publicised books of all time.

2 My brother decided he needed a qualification, in his .... , a degree in engineering.
I'm shocked by what you've just told me, and if that's really the .... , I shall resign.
To the jury, it sounded like a straightforward .... of intimidation.

3 I'd like to .... a bit more money if I could, because the cost of living is rising all the time.
I've been asked to .... a speech when Anna gets her music prize.
So what do you .... of everything going on at the school at the moment?

4 I didn't think Astrid Bergman's portrayal of the princess was .... and it spoilt the film.
Mark had no difficulty........................... students at top universities that they should apply for a job with his company on graduation.
The President put forward such a .... argument for change that no one opposed him.

5 I don't think there's any .... in trying to find a solution to the problem at this stage.
There didn't seem to be much .... to what he was saying.
Stella was hoping to get her project finished, but she'd been working all day, and at that .... she decided to stop.

Use of English Part 5

For questions 1–8, complete the second sentence so that it has a similar meaning to the first sentence, using the word given. Do not change the word given. You must use between three and six words, including the word given. Here is an example (0).

0 I've never been at all interested in learning to play a musical instrument.
SLIGHTEST

I've never *had the slightest interest in* learning to play a musical instrument.

1 Anna's fed up with the company and she's intending to leave work as soon as she can.
NO

Anna's fed up with the company and she's got *no intention of staying* longer than she has to.

2 Susan picked the baby up gently, because she didn't want to wake him.
TO

Susan picked the baby up gently so *as not to wake* him.

3 They were able to creep away unobserved because it was very dark.
OWING

They were able to creep away unobserved *owing to the fact that* it was very dark.

4 The car was redesigned and, as a result, sales rose rapidly.
RESULTED

The successful redesigning of the car *resulted in a rapid rise* in sales.

5 Despite improving his performance, Smith is still not in the top three for the 10,000 metres.
LED

The improvement in Smith's performance *has not led him to be* in the top three for the 10,000 metres.

6 We should leave about six, otherwise we might not get there in time for dinner.
SET

If *we don't set off about* six, we might not get there in time for dinner.

7 You should make the sauce thicker if you want to improve the flavour.
THICKEN

You'll *thicken the sauce* in order to improve the flavour.

8 After several years, heavy traffic caused the bridge to collapse.
DUE

The collapse *of the bridge was due to* several years of heavy traffic.

Listening Part 3

3 You will hear an interview with an Irish-Australian writer and broadcaster called Patrick O'Reilly who writes in the Irish-Gaelic language. For questions 1–6, choose the answer (A, B, C or D) which fits best according to what you hear.

1 Why is the Irish language significant to Patrick?

  A It was spoken to him when he was a child.
  B It evokes city life in a particular era.
  C It came close to disappearing at one time.
  D It is a major part of his cultural heritage.

2 Which aspect of Irish has particularly impressed Patrick?

  A its age as a language
  B its suitability for song lyrics
  C its success in the modern world
  D its role in broadcasting

3 Why was Patrick keen to learn Irish?

  A He lacked a strong identity as an Australian.
  B He was reacting against other people's views.
  C He was aware that it would broaden his horizons.
  D He wanted to be actively involved in its revival.

4 According to Patrick, what makes Irish different from other languages in Australia?

  A It is impossible to show how it sounds.
  B It is not a language published in Australia.
  C It is used as a second language.
  D It has not gone through a process of evolution.

5 What reason does Patrick give for Irish becoming fashionable?

  A Speaking languages fluently has become a status symbol.
  B It is associated with the popularity of the country.
  C It is seen as the language of popular fairy tales.
  D Many Irish-Australians now aspire to live in Ireland.

Gaelic /ˈgeɪ.lɪk, gæl.ɪk/ *noun* [U] a language spoken in parts of Ireland, Scotland and, in the past, the Isle of Man • **Gaelic** *adjective*

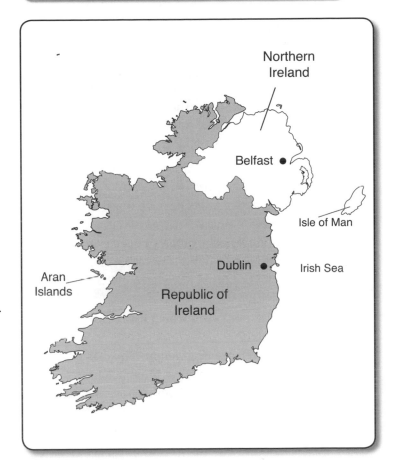

6 What does Patrick say about other people's explanations of why they are learning Irish?

  A They may not reveal the whole truth.
  B They show they are trying to reassure themselves.
  C They reveal a lack of self-awareness.
  D They indicate that people feel little need to justify themselves.

Unit 3 All in the mind

Grammar
The passive

❶ ⓐ ⊙ Look at these sentences written by CAE students, some of which contain mistakes in the use of the passive or in the tense of the passive verb. Find the mistake and correct it or put a tick if the sentence is correct.

1 The fact that women work in the same jobs as men has been well accepted in my country. ✓

2 The role of women has been changed a lot since my grandmother's times.

3 The work experience programme was given opportunities to hundreds of teenagers.

4 I was lucky because I have been given a lift to school nearly every day.

5 The English course on which I was enrolled has now finished.

6 Many children are overweight. This has been happened because they eat too much junk food.

7 The book has been written three years ago by Jemma Paige, a Canadian historian.

8 Once the journey time has been calculated, we'll know when to set off.

9 I've enjoyed using the library since it is modernised.

10 This situation has been caused by negligence.

11 I was looking forward to the trip but it has been cancelled at the last moment.

12 The ring Evita often wore in public has been auctioned off for a large sum of money.

13 Mount Jiree has been thought to be thousands of years old, but no one is sure.

14 The whole concept of sport has been changed in people's minds.

15 The beauty of the beach has been adversely affected by tourism.

ⓑ Look at sentences 1–15 again and decide which of the incorrect sentences:

• had passive verbs in the wrong tense? ....
• needed an active verb not a passive one? ....

❷ Read this extract from an article and then put the words in brackets into the correct order, using the appropriate form of the passive.

SLEEP AND DREAMS

Although they have been a topic of speculation throughout human history, the content and purpose of dreams **(1)** _are not understood_ (not/understand). It **(2)** .... (now/acknowledge) that dreams **(3)** .... (strongly/link) to the rapid eye movement that takes place during the first stage of sleep. Over the full course of a typical human lifespan, a total approaching six years may **(4)** .... (spend) dreaming. Yet, despite this, it **(5)** .... (not/establish) where in the brain dreams originate, or whether they have a common cause.

Philosophers and artists **(6)** .... (for centuries/fascinate) by sleep and dreams. Yet they **(7)** .... (often/portray) as a dark and often disturbing sphere of human existence, despite the fact that it **(8)** .... (know/for many years) that both physical survival and mental wellbeing depend upon them.

Two thousand years ago, dreams **(9)** .... (regularly/interpret) as supernatural or divine communication, and they **(10)** .... (therefore/think) to foretell the future. By the beginning of the twentieth century, the interpretation of dreams **(11)** .... (most commonly/associate) with psychoanalysis and its famous practitioners, Freud and Jung, who regarded dreams as the bridge between the unconscious and conscious mind, a tool with which the secrets of the human mind could **(12)** .... (finally/unlock). But the key to those secrets has **(13)** .... (yet/find).

Vocabulary

Word building

The following words are all in Unit 3 of the Student's Book.

1 Make the abstract nouns formed from these base words.

> recognise *recognition* able critic relation evolve
> apt

2 Name the people associated with these nouns.

> architecture *architect* science novel psychology
> education philosophy paint

3 Make the adjective(s) formed from these nouns.

> mind *mindless* nature science point intuition
> character stress

4 Make the adverbs formed from these base words.

> critic *critically* nature science increase character

Writing

CAE writing tasks

1 a ⊙ Read the openings of seven different writing tasks written by CAE students and then match them with the correct description below.

a	article	e	proposal
b	competition entry	f	report
c	contribution to a book/magazine	g	review
d	letter of application		

1 ....

I am writing in response to your advertisement in the local paper. I am a 21 year-old girl from Denmark who is currently working in England with disabled and elderly people. I like my job very much, but as my contract runs out soon, I need to find a new post.

2 ....

Do you realize that If nothing is done to prevent it, the air which we all breathe, might kill us in the near future? Do you care enough about your own health and the health of the next generations to help in an efficient way to protect the environment in which we all live?

3 ....

It will be interesting to read about what other people say is popular in different countries. In China, a popular TV programme is a soap series called *Wild Swans*, which is on at 7.30pm every night after the national news. It is about the history of a Chinese family, through three generations and across 100 years.

4 ....

Introduction

My aim is to outline the current use of cars and highlight the alternative means of transport available. I also consider some recommendations for future developments of transport.

5 ....

This is my essay about innovations. I have never tried anything like this before, but I'd love to win a prize. The two innovations that have really benefited me most are credit cards and personal stereos. I do not leave my house without these two smart things.

6 ....

Picking the right computer out of a thousand choices can indeed be quite a difficult task. That is why we will compare two somewhat similar games and help you figure out which one you like best.

7 ....

The number of families living in the city of Zurich has dropped. The two main factors are the lack of apartments at an affordable price and unsuitable transport facilities. The present aim is to identify effective measures to make Zurich a desirable and attractive place to raise a family and suggest how they can be introduced.

b Which task:

a contains a heading?
b is a first attempt at something?
c is obviously one of several similar pieces?
d uses direct questions?
e involves comparison?
f describes someone's work experiences?
g intends to give practical ideas to solve a housing problem?

Reading Part 1

You are going to read three extracts which are all concerned in some way with psychology. For questions 1–6, choose the answer (A, B, C or D) which you think best fits according to the text.

The Cocktail Party Effect

Think back to the last party you went to. Somehow you managed to filter out all the other conversations you could hear around you and tune into the person talking to you. Then suddenly you heard your name mentioned across the room and your ears pricked up. What were they saying about you?

Our ability to filter out unwanted sounds and then register them when they become important to us is fascinating. How can we unblock them the moment someone mentions our name? This phenomenon was dubbed the Cocktail Party Effect by scientist Colin Cherry back in 1953. He investigated it by giving volunteers headphones, playing a different message into each ear, and instructing them to repeat aloud everything they heard from one of the voices. He found that even if they were played two simultaneous recordings of the same voice, they could only attend to one message. In fact, people were so good at shutting out the second voice that if he played the message backwards or switched it into a different language they didn't notice. He decided that we focus on one voice by observing a combination of its pitch, volume and the direction it's coming from.

So how are we able to switch focus when we hear certain words? It seems that some words are 'flagged up' in our minds as being particularly significant, so whenever we hear them we pay attention. Warnings such as 'Fire!' or 'Mind your head' are registered instantly, but by far the most effective is the mention of our name.

1 Which of these conclusions did Cherry come to?

A People will ignore information if it is in a foreign language.

B People find background noise distracting.

C People respond to a more attractive voice.

D People can distinguish the particular features of one voice.

Book Review:
What is Intelligence? *James R. Flynn*

line 1 This is a mystery story – and an intriguing one. In the early 1980s, the author made the startling discovery that, over the course of the twentieth century and across the developed world, IQ tests had shown big gains from one generation to the next, a phenomenon that had previously gone unnoticed because until then test scores were continually 'normalised' to keep the mean at 100. So if people are becoming more intelligent, why are we not struck by the extraordinary cleverness of our children or the stupidity of our parents?

In his book, Flynn seeks to explain this. He argues that IQ tests are made up of sub-tests measuring a range of cognitive skills. People's overall scores have shot up, not because they

2 What does the writer conclude about the fact that people always respond to their name?

A It shows that people emphasise names more than other words.

B It requires alertness and conscious effort on the part of the listener.

C It is something everyone is psychologically programmed to do.

D It occurs because people like having their sense of identity reinforced.

are doing any better at basic skills they learn in the classroom, but because their scores have improved in the tests measuring conceptual thinking and on-the-spot problem-solving.

Flynn attributes this to changes in society. Before 1900, most people had few years at school and then worked long hours doing repetitive jobs in factories, shops or agriculture. They had little opportunity or need for conceptual thinking; their minds were focused on practical matters. Now we have mass secondary education and large numbers of people go into responsible jobs, where they are required to think for themselves. With more education comes a thirst for books and the arts and since the 1950s, we have seen the emergence of a new visual culture. Our brain capacity has not grown, but we are using the capacity we have in more imaginative ways.

3 What is the 'mystery story' that the writer refers to in line 1?

   A why scientists adjusted IQ test scores before the 1980s
   B why skills learnt in the classroom are not improving
   C why having a visual culture has a major impact on intelligence
   D why people's cleverness appears to remain constant across the generations

4 What conclusion has Flynn reached about intelligence?

   A People are more intelligent than they were in the 1950s.
   B Children today are more intelligent than their parents.
   C People today have developed new ways of thinking.
   D Children are more intelligent because they receive a broader education.

What's in a Face?

In a world of six billion people, every face is unique. And John Cleese, actor, author and comedian, his own face famous to millions the world over as Basil in *Fawlty Towers*, is fascinated by this uniqueness – how the face marks us out as surely as our fingerprints, and how it affects the way we communicate with and relate to others. His four-part series exploring *The Human Face* is an ambitious mix of science, psychology, culture and comic sketches. The series is the definitive guide to the history of the face, exploring identity, beauty, expressions and fame with the help of scientific experts and a few famous faces from the world of acting.

Over the course of the series, Cleese sets out to unravel the mysteries of identity, perception, creativity and sexuality hidden behind the mask of the human face. 'And at the same time,' he adds, 'there are plenty of little jokes. We're not trying for laugh-out-loud funny, but we're trying to put information across in a humorous way. The idea was that the four aspects we should pay attention to were beauty, facial expressions, fame – because if you're famous, people know your face – and a very interesting one that's more difficult to describe, which is about identity. To what extent are we our faces? How much do our faces really tell people about us? The programme about facial expressions is intriguing because it shows how we misread people's expressions, particularly whether we are lying or not.'

5 Which point does the writer make in the first paragraph?

   A Well-known actors played a major part in the making of Cleese's series.
   B Cleese has tried to combine too many different elements in the series.
   C Cleese realises that the individual nature of each face impacts on human psychology.
   D The series is based on the fact that Cleese's face is recognised internationally.

6 How does Cleese feel about the series now it is complete?

   A He is certain that his use of humour has been successful.
   B He thinks that the content of one of the programmes is hard to define.
   C He believes that one programme will prove more popular than the others.
   D He is fascinated by the concept of fame that it portrays.

Listening Part 1

(4) **You will hear three different extracts. For questions 1–6, choose the answer (A, B or C) which fits best according to what you hear. There are two questions for each extract.**

Extract One

You overhear two friends talking about an incident one of them has seen.

1 What happened to the woman's car?
  A It was badly scratched when a lorry reversed.
  B It was completely destroyed when a lorry drove over it.
  C It escaped damage when a lorry turned round.

2 How did the woman react to what had happened?
  A She was disappointed about missing her day out.
  B She felt some sympathy for the lorry driver.
  C She was extremely angry with the lorry driver.

Extract Two

You will hear part of an interview with a zoo director who is talking about the orang-utans at the zoo.

3 How did visitors at the zoo react to Marla's escape?
  A They were curious and crowded round to watch Marla.
  B They were worried about Marla and offered her food.
  C They were frightened because Marla posed a threat.

4 Which of Marla's actions does the zoo director find particularly clever?
  A managing to hide some keys
  B using sign cards in an appropriate way
  C understanding why the vet had arrived

Extract Three

On the radio, you hear two people talking about a stonemason.

5 What was the stonemason's response to the people around him?
  A He felt stopping work to speak to them was a waste of time.
  B He was apparently at first unaware of their presence.
  C He was willing to describe his skills and techniques.

6 How do the speakers interpret the onlookers' fascination with the stonemason's work?
  A They wrongly believe this kind of work pays well.
  B They value craft work because it has become fashionable.
  C They find working with technology rather unsatisfying.

Grammar

Expressing possibility, probability and certainty

❶ **Choose the correct modal verb in each sentence.**

1 When you choose a book for a child to read, it *can't/* *shouldn't* be too difficult for their age.

2 Katerina knew it *can't/couldn't* be Igor ringing the doorbell because he had a key.

3 When the new students arrived, there was nobody to welcome them and this *mustn't/shouldn't* have happened.

4 If you give Angelo the news now it *could/must* upset him, so tell him later on.

5 Jack isn't here yet so he *must/should* be waiting for Rose who's always late.

6 According to the directions, the hotel *could/should* have been next to the park but there was only a garage there.

7 If we offer free sandwiches, it *can/may* encourage more people to attend the lecture.

8 We are looking for people who *might/should* be able to write reviews for the magazine.

❷ ⑤ **Read what a student said about the photographs of the two offices below and then choose the correct word. Then listen and check your answers.**

'There are quite a lot of people working close together in the first office. It **(1)** *could/* *must* be a newspaper office but it's difficult to tell what kind of business it is. It **(2)** *can't / must* be on the ground floor because there's a lot of light coming in so it's highly **(3)** *likely / possible* that it's in an office block. There are two men standing up. They're **(4)** *probably / possibly* not too busy as they seem quite relaxed. The man on the right **(5)** *can't / might* be the boss as he's telling the other man something. The second photograph is in a much quieter office. The two men **(6)** *can't / must* be working on some designs together. They **(7)** *can't / might* be architects or designers. They **(8)** *can't / must* be discussing something connected to the designs. They **(9)** *might / must* well have come across a problem but it seems **(10)** *impossible / unlikely* to be a serious one as they don't look very worried.'

Vocabulary

Adjective/noun collocations

❶ ⓐ Match an adjective on the left to a noun on the right to make a suitable collocation.

flexible	contract
heavy	discussion
large	number
informal	possibility
poor	range
strong	working conditions
temporary	working hours
wide	workload

ⓑ Now read the adverts below and then complete the gaps, using a suitable collocation from exercise 1a. You will sometimes need to add a(n) or the.

Past graduates have gone on to **(1)** .... *a wide range* ......
of jobs in different areas of the computer industry.
If you are interested in doing this course, phone to
arrange a time for **(2)** .... with the
course leader. This will give you the opportunity to ask
questions so you are sure it's the right course for you.

At IMG International we put our employees first. We
know that a leading cause of stress in some industries is
trying to deal with **(3)** .... under
(4) .... We will expect you to work
hard during your contracted hours but in return we
offer a comfortable working environment with a sports
club and subsidised canteen. For parents with young
children **(5)** .... can be an option.

During the summer months, Hotel Excel
employs **(6)** .... of extra staff
in its establishments around the country. We
can offer you **(7)** .... for six
months initially. If you are hard-working, there is
(8) .... that we can find you work
in our hotels in other parts of the world for the
winter months.

work and job

❷ Complete the gaps in these sentences, using *work* or *job*.

1 I like outdoor ......*work*...... so I'm applying for a job
   as a tour guide.

2 If you want to get a good .... in a
   multinational company, you'll probably have to get
   through several interviews.

3 As people climb the promotion ladder, they tend
   to spend longer and longer at .... as their
   responsibilities increase.

4 I really like living in Sydney so I'm planning to
   find .... here.

5 I'm going to do a full-time course so I'm leaving
   my .... at the health club at the end of the
   week.

6 I'd like to accept the .... of deputy manager
   offered to me in your email received yesterday.

Formation of adverbs

**❸ ⓐ Make adverbs from these adjectives. There is
one adjective that cannot be made into an adverb.**

actual.*ly*.......	basic	complete.............
full.............	general.............	likely.............
necessary.............	private.............	public.............
satisfactory.............	shy.............	suitable.............
terrible.............	tragic.............	true.............
whole.............		

**ⓑ Now match the adjective endings with the rules
for forming adverbs and then complete the table
with the words from exercise 3a.**

Adjectives ending in:	Rules	Examples	Exceptions
-l	usually drop -e and add -y	*actually, generally*	*fully*
-le	usually keep -e and add -ly		
-e	usually add -ly		
-ly	usually add -ally		
-y	cannot be made into an adverb		
-ic	usually drop -y and add -ily		

Writing
Functional phrases

Match the useful phrases on the right to a function on the left. Some functions have more than one phrase.

Giving an opinion	**A** To sum up
	B Some people argue that ... but others
Persuading	**C** In my point of view
	D I would be grateful if you could let me know
Summarising	**E** The benefits of doing this are
	F I would be more than happy to
Comparing and contrasting	**G** The main advantage for you is
	H In conclusion,
Recommending and advising	**I** On the one hand ... On the other hand
	J It would be a good idea to
Asking for advice or help	**K** I would like to know what
	L I think it would definitely
Making an offer	**M** An essential feature of ... is
Describing	

Use of English Part 3

For questions 1–10, read the text below. Use the word given in capitals at the end of some of the lines to form a word that fits in the gap in the same line. There is an example at the beginning (0).

Putting some fun into the workplace

A study of 737 chief executives of major corporations found that 98 per cent would hire someone with a good sense of humour in (0) ......preference...... to someone who seemed to lack one. **PREFER**

Having fun at work also inspires (1) .....Loyalty..... in employees. According to a survey of 1,000 workers, those who rated their manager's sense of humour 'above average' said there was a 90 per cent (2) .....probability.....that they would remain in their job for more than a year. If they worked for a boss whose sense of humour they described as 'average' or 'below', the employee's (3) .....Likelihood..... of staying dropped to 77 per cent. **LOYAL** **PROBABLE** **LIKELY**

So laughter is (4) .....beneficial.....and good for business. This knowledge could, however, add to the stress of (5) .....applicants..... when they are interviewed if making jokes doesn't come naturally to them. But being funny doesn't (6) .....necessarily..... mean being a stand-up (7) .....comedian..... . The important thing is to strive for a light-hearted atmosphere in the workplace. **BENEFIT** **APPLY** **NECESSARY** **COMEDY**

There is, (8) .....fortunately....., a downside to all this. For instance, some people working in retail jobs are required to smile (9) .....continually..... . Such enforced happiness can apparently cause (10) .....dissatisfaction..... at work and result in emotional stress. **FORTUNE** **CONTINUE** **SATISFY**

Use of English Part 5

For questions 1–8, complete the second sentence so that it has a similar meaning to the first sentence, using the word given. Do not change the word given. You must use between three and six words, including the word given. Here is an example (0).

0 I do not intend to stay in my present job very much longer.
NO
I have ...... *no intention of staying* ...... in my present job very much longer.

1 There is a strong possibility that the manager will choose Antonio to play on Saturday but it depends on his state of fitness.
WELL
Antonio ... *is well likely* ... the manager to play on Saturday but it depends on his state of fitness.

2 We are sure that the government's new policy will successfully reduce unemployment.
BOUND
We think that the government's new policy ... *is bound to succeed* ... in reducing unemployment.

3 You can't blame Sam for breaking the window because he wasn't even here this morning.
BEEN
It ... *can't have been* ... *Sam who* broke the window because he wasn't even here this morning.

4 It is not likely that the effects of global warming can be reversed.
LIKELIHOOD
There is ... *little likelihood of* ... reversing the effects of global warming.

5 Some people tend to do better in a pressurised working environment.
CONSTANT
Some people work better when they are ... *under* *constant* *pressure at* work.

6 I gave up the job at the hotel because there were too few challenges.
ENOUGH
I gave up the job at the hotel because it ... *was not challenging enough for* me.

7 There isn't as much space in this new office as there was in the old one.
SPACIOUS
This new office is ... *as much spacious as* ... the old one.

8 My boss doesn't allow us to eat at our desks.
LINE
My boss draws ... *a line about eating* *against* ... at our desks.

Listening Part 4

06 You will hear five short extracts in which people are talking about their jobs.

TASK ONE

For questions **1–5**, choose from the list **(A–H)** each speaker's job.

TASK TWO

For questions **6–10**, choose from the list **(A–H)** what each speaker says they enjoy most about their job.

While you listen you must complete both tasks.

A air traffic controller
B engineer
C fashion buyer
D interior designer
E museum director
F shop assistant
G lawyer
H website designer

Speaker 1 [| **1**]
Speaker 2 [| **2**]
Speaker 3 [| **3**]
Speaker 4 [| **4**]
Speaker 5 [| **5**]

A extending existing skills
B doing accounts
C keeping regular hours
D managing staff
E meeting new people
F satisfying customers
G travelling abroad
H working as a team

Speaker 1 [| **6**]
Speaker 2 [| **7**]
Speaker 3 [| **8**]
Speaker 4 [| **9**]
Speaker 5 [| **10**]

Grammar

Infinitives and verb + -ing forms

❶ **Read this extract from a biography and then complete the gaps with an infinitive or verb + -ing form, using the verb in brackets.**

Ranulph Fiennes is a man who isn't afraid of (1) .....*pushing*..... (push) himself to the limits. He's famous for (2) .... (visit) both the North and South Poles by land between 1979 and 1982 and (3) .... (cross) the Antarctic on foot in 1993.

In 2000 he attempted (4) .... (reach) the North Pole on his own at the age of 55. On that trip, there was too much food and equipment for a single sledge (5) .... (transport), so he took two. This meant (6) .... (walk) one mile forward with the first sledge, then (7) .... (go) back for the second one so every mile gained involved (8) .... (travel) three on the ground. To do such a trip with one sledge is dangerous enough, but it is much worse with two. (9) .... (park) the first sledge, you then have to set off (10) .... (fetch) the second one but if conditions get worse, however hard you try (11) .... (find) it, you may never see it again. Fiennes didn't ever lose his sledges in the snow but at one point during the journey, they fell through weak ice and he was forced (12) .... (pull) them out by hand. He would have kept (13) .... (go) but he got frostbite in his fingers which made it impossible for him (14) .... (carry on).

The experiences Fiennes had that time discouraged him from (15) .... (make) another attempt but he was not ready to stop (16) .... (push) himself to the limits. Since then he has carried out the extraordinary feat of (17) .... (complete) seven marathons in seven days on seven continents and in 2005 succeeded in (18) .... (reach) 8,690m in an attempt to climb Everest.

❷ **Read each pair of sentences and then answer the question which follows.**

1   **A**   I forgot to take change for the bus fare.
     B   I'll never forget going in an aeroplane for the first time.

In which sentence did the speaker fail to do something? ......A.....

2   **A**   Jessie didn't stop complaining about her legs aching until she saw the view from the top of the hill.
     B   When we'd walked halfway up the hill, I stopped to admire the view.

In which sentence did someone stop for a purpose? ....

3   **A**   I tried to tell Simon but I just couldn't.
     B   I tried sailing but I didn't like it.

In which sentence did someone attempt something difficult? ....

4   **A**   The woman who used to live in the basement below us went on to become a famous writer.
     B   My uncle went on playing professional football until he was nearly 40.

In which sentence did something continue for a period of time? ....

5   **A**   The college regrets to inform students that their results will be delayed by a week.
     B   The students regret not paying more attention during classes.

Which sentence is looking back at something that has already happened? ....

Vocabulary
Compound nouns

❶ ⓐ Complete this crossword puzzle.

ACROSS

2 The building I live in used to have a .... on the ground floor selling hats.

3 My twin brother always takes my .... in any family arguments, even if I'm in the wrong.

4 I don't have .... to phone Rob before I leave – it's already four o'clock.

7 A new footbridge has been built over the railway ....

8 In American English, autumn is known as the ....

11 After about 2004, most computers were sold with a flat ....

12 If you go .... off the Great Barrier Reef in Australia, you will see beautiful corals, fish and sponges under the water.

13 The new lamp gave off a really bright ....

day: *daytime* ....
wind: ....
water: ....
sky: ....
work: ....

DOWN

1 It was so hot last night, I had a single .... on the bed rather than a duvet.

5 Grain used to be ground into flour in a .... powered by wind or water.

6 We have a 15-minute .... between classes.

8 The .... of the wind made it very hard to stand up on the clifftop.

9 What he told us was a .... of rubbish.

10 If you lose your board when you're .... you need to be able to swim to the beach.

ⓑ Some nouns are made from two other nouns, e.g. *letterbox, workmate*. Make new nouns with *day*, *wind*, *water*, *sky*, and *work*, using the words from the crossword puzzle in exercise 1a and write them underneath the puzzle. You may use any noun more than once.

Phrasal verbs with *take*

❷ Read these groups of sentences and then complete the gaps with the correct adverb or preposition.

1 a The waiter took our plates .... as soon as we had finished.

b Do you want to take your sandwich .... or eat it here?

c I'm no good at mental arithmetic – I took 46 .... from 102 and got 54 which is wrong!

2 a My new laptop isn't working properly so I'll have to take it ....

b When I hear a song by The Spice Girls on the radio it always takes me .... to when I was a little girl.

c I take .... what I said earlier. I wasn't thinking and I didn't mean it.

3 a Sabrina got the sack because she'd taken too many days ....

b Tourism has really taken .... on the island but prices have risen too.

c Sabrina tried to cheer herself up by taking herself .... on a short holiday to Turkey.

4 a To feel healthier, you should give up junk food and take .... a sport.

b Replying to emails can take .... a lot of time.

c I have decided to take .... the place you offered me at your college.

Reading Part 2

You are going to read an extract from an article about a sport. Six paragraphs have been removed from the extract. Choose from the paragraphs A–G the one which fits each gap (1–6). There is one extra paragraph which you do not need to use.

THE SCARIEST RIDE ON THE PLANET

Charles Starmer-Smith spent a weekend in Norway learning how to ride on a bob skeleton, a one-person sledge like a tin tray which races down an ice track at 60mph.

I glanced down at the red snow by my feet just a few yards from the finishing gate of the Lillehammer bob skeleton track. The bob skeleton is also known as a toboggan and reminded me of a tray a waiter might use to bring plates of food out in a restaurant. But this one was going to have me on it rather than a pile of food so seeing the blood of an earlier rider was a little unnerving. Make no bones about it, this has to be one of the scariest rides on the planet.

1

I feigned nonchalance at this information, but I was fooling no one. I have made a habit of scaring myself: I've leapt down the face of Switzerland's Verzasca Dam – the world's biggest bungee jump, I have descended the near-vertical Corbets Couloir at Jacksonhole – perhaps the most fearsome ski run in North America – and I have learnt to ski-jump at Calgary.

2

At least I was not alone as several other novices would be joining me. After a fitful sleep, we went out early to walk to the top of the track. The snow, hanging heavy on the branches of Lillehammer's forested slopes, made the track look even more imposing. Snaking down the slope like a giant metallic python, the walls were steeper, the straights were longer but the 16 turns were much sharper than I expected.

3

Halfway up, we arrived at the infamous Turn 13, a shuddering 180-degree U-turn where the centrifugal pressures equal those experienced by fighter pilots. 'This is where you'll feel the full force,' said Tony, our instructor, his eyes sparkling. 'So, is the track running quickly?' I asked tentatively. He did not need to answer.

4

All we caught was a flash of eyeballs and overalls as the rider sliced around the curved wall of ice at breathtaking speed. We glanced at each other, panic etched across our faces and laughed the nervous laugh of the truly terrified as we realized this would soon be us.

5

I therefore took comfort in the knowledge that, with a professional in charge, someone would be keeping his head while the rest of us were losing ours. I drew the short straw and was given position four, where you feel the full brunt of the force with nothing but cool Norwegian air behind you.

6

We barely had time to check that we were all in one piece before we were sent off to get kitted up for the skeleton. On Tony's instructions I lay face down on the sledge, arms clamped by my sides, nose inches from the ice and off I went. After seventy seconds of terror, I could barely speak and my body felt as though it had been in a boxing ring, but I had never felt so alive. What a ride!

A Before we had any more time to contemplate our fate, we found ourselves at the top, climbing aboard a bobraft. Designed to give you a feel for the track before going down on your own, this giant, padded open-top box looked about as aerodynamic as a bus, but it travelled a whole lot faster. It had a driver who did this all the time which was reassuring.

B As if on cue, snow crystals began to jump in unison on the metallic railings as, high above, a sledge began its inexorable journey down. What started as a distant hum became a rattle, then a roar as the sledge reached top speed. The tarpaulin covering the track stiffened in its wake and the girders groaned.

C On these previous occasions, I had had experience or the expertise of others to fall back on, but with this there was nothing from which to draw strength. The bob skeleton confounds conventional logic.

D It started deceptively slowly, but within moments picked up speed. It soon became clear that the rider has little control and survival instinct takes over.

E It is hard to describe the debilitating effect that such immense speeds and forces have on your body. It was like nothing I have ever experienced. The last thing I remember going through my mind was straining just to keep my head upright.

F We listened to advice on how to get round them safely — use your eyes to steer and tilt your head away from the corners to minimize the pressure. It sounded simple enough, but get it wrong at these speeds and your chin faces the cheese-grater.

G The man behind these adrenalin-packed weekends at Norway's Olympic park, explained that those who attempt the famous run often accidentally "kiss" the ice with their nose or chin, leaving a layer or three of skin behind.

Listening Part 3

🎧 You will hear a radio interview with a woman called Sarah who was rescued from a sinking yacht. For questions 1–6, choose the answer (A, B, C or D) which fits best according to what you hear.

1 What was the weather like when Sarah and the others set out?

   A as they had anticipated
   B like it had been the day before
   C better than on the outward journey
   D showing signs of improvement

2 What first made Sarah realise that something was wrong?

   A She felt a sudden movement.
   B She heard someone shout.
   C She heard something tearing.
   D She saw something fall into the water.

3 Sarah and Peter decided to turn back rather than continue because

   A the crew were getting tired.
   B the boat was leaking.
   C it was a shorter distance to cover.
   D they followed the advice they were given.

4 What problem did they have when the tanker arrived?

   A The plane had given the wrong position.
   B They weren't visible.
   C It came too close to them.
   D Their flares wouldn't work.

5 Why were there difficulties with the small rescue boat?

   A The four men were too heavy for it.
   B It was brought up too fast.
   C The people holding it weren't strong enough.
   D It hadn't been fixed to the rope carefully enough.

6 What mistake does Sarah now realise she made during the rescue?

   A trying to save as many valuables as possible
   B underestimating the difficulty of climbing a rope ladder
   C letting the others be rescued first
   D trying to save the boat from sinking

Grammar
Avoiding repetition

Read this book review of *The Thirteenth Tale* and then complete the gaps, using the reference words from the box on the right.

all	both	~~first~~	neither	none	one	one of	these
those during which following what this which
including whose for herself her own herself
of her own living there it is through

REVIEW

The Thirteenth Tale *by Diane Setterfield*

This gripping novel, Diane Setterfield's **(1)** ....*first*...., could best be described as a mystery story. Margaret Lee, a young biographer, is summoned by Vida Winter, a novelist of considerable renown, to write her biography. It is **(2)** .... sets Margaret on a voyage of discovery, not only about Vida's life, but about **(3)** ....

Vida had led a secretive and reclusive life, **(4)** .... she has created many outlandish life histories **(5)** .... , all of them pure fantasy. It is only as she comes to the end of her life that she feels able to expose the secrets of her past. Margaret travels to Vida's home in Yorkshire, **(6)** .... with Vida while she writes the biography. As a biographer, Margaret deals in fact not fiction, so as Vida tells her story, Margaret embarks on research **(7)** .... to establish the truth. **(8)** .... the coming together of **(9)** .... two accounts that the reader gradually discovers how the eminent author has kept the family secrets and made a success of her life **(10)** .... can only be described as a very disturbed childhood.

Vida's tale is **(11)** .... gothic strangeness featuring the Angelfield family headed by the beautiful but unstable Isabelle. Her twin daughters, **(12)** .... bizarre behaviour brings havoc to **(13)** .... around them are called Adeline and Emmeline. It soon becomes apparent from the twins' behaviour that **(14)** .... is capable of leading a normal life, and when the house they live in is deliberately set alight one night, it seems at first that **(15)** .... the girls have perished in the fire.

As Margaret gradually unravels the truth about Vida, it becomes apparent that **(16)** .... of the people involved with the twins, **(17)** .... the housekeeper and the gardener, escaped unscathed, so the story is to a large extent **(18)** .... of tragedy. But by the end of the novel, **(19)** .... is resolved and even the smallest of details in Vida's story has its place. Meanwhile, there is a hint that Margaret **(20)** .... is about to find a happy ending.

Vocabulary
Adjective/noun collocations

1 a Match an adjective on the top row to a noun on the bottom row. Some adjectives match more than one noun.

classical   considerable   deafening   detailed   fashionable   gripping   hazardous   instant   public   random

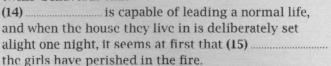

image   noise   story   amount   feedback   order   music   description   journey   clothing

b Complete the gaps, using collocations from exercise 1a on page 31.

1 Most teachers think it is important to give students *instant feedback* when they have done a presentation.

2 I was unable to sleep last night due to the .... coming out of the club down the road.

3 Many film stars have a .... which is at odds with their private life.

4 I've never seen my sister wearing .... ; the way she dresses is often bizarre.

5 James put a .... of time and effort into his project, only to be told that it needed rewriting.

6 I was taken aback because most of the books in the library seemed to be in completely .... and as a result I couldn't find what I was looking for.

7 We had an unexpectedly .... across the States last year as there were flash floods.

8 We all loved the book; it was such a .... that none of us could put it down.

9 The witness managed to give the police such a .... of the thief that they were able to identify him from police records.

10 I've always enjoyed listening to .... if I want to relax and unwind.

❷ Complete the gaps, using the most suitable adverb from the boxes below.

harshly	negatively	highly	~~widely~~

When the film was first released it was clear that opinions about it would differ **(1)** .... *widely* .... The critics raved about it, praising the acting **(2)** .... But audiences responded **(3)** .... to it, criticising the plot **(4)** .... and savaging the performance of the leading actor.

hungrily	tightly	silently	contentedly

In the first scene, Peter creeps **(5)** .... down the corridor to his little sister's room and leaves her birthday present on the bed. Susanna smiles **(6)** .... when she sees the tiny teddy bear and she is still clutching it **(7)** .... in her hand when she goes downstairs and **(8)** .... gobbles up the breakfast her mother has prepared.

Synonyms

❸ The words in the box are all synonyms of the adjectives below. Match the words with their synonyms.

~~absorbing~~	awesome	complicated
gripping	marvellous	demanding
intriguing	complex	engaging
stunning	incredible	problematic
stimulating	challenging	amazing

difficult: ....

interesting: ...*absorbing*................................

wonderful: ....

Writing
Correcting your writing

⊙ Read this competition entry written by a CAE student. Find and correct 16 errors in the writing.

WHAT WOULD YOU PUT IN A TIME CAPSULE TO BE OPENED IN 100 YEARS' TIME?

The first thing I would to suggest is a book, it has lots of drawings and pictures. These should be showing our civilisation, our traditions and culture. Pictures of people at home, at school or at work are good examples of things to be including. Because of English is one of the most popular language in the world, I would also suggest to describe these pictures with a text in English. Secondly, I believe that clothing, fashion and design are important ways of showing how a society is like. However I would like to recommend include a traditional white wedding dress in the capsule, since to get married is a special event in one's life. This is the reason what I think people in the future will find an original wedding dress interesting. My final suggestion is a computer because of the major influence on our modern society. It not only represents modern technology and our development, but also the way by which we live and work today. I hope you should find my competition entry interesting and to read it carefully.

Use of English Part 1

For questions 1–12, read the text below and decide which answer (A, B, C or D) best fits each gap. There is an example at the beginning (0).

THE KOGOD COURTYARD

At the Smithsonian Institute in Washington, the most striking (0) ...... c ...... of the new Kogod courtyard is its canopy roof. The existing walls at the Smithsonian were not strong enough to (1) .... the weight of a ceiling so, instead, the vast undulating glass roof is (2) .... by eight aluminium columns, and carefully designed to (3) .... in with the original stonework. The wave-like structure, the first of its (4) .... in the world, is constructed of deep, diamond-shaped glass panes, packed around the sides with (5) .... cotton from denim jeans to (6) .... as sound insulation. This (7) .... conditions near perfect for musical performances in the courtyard.

From inside the courtyard, clouds and aircraft are clearly (8) .... through the canopy. But closer inspection reveals a milky surface covered in enamel dots, which (9) .... about two thirds of the light, (10) .... helping to keep the courtyard cool during the baking hot Washington summers.

Water is also a vital element of the design. When no event is being held, a wafer-thin 'river' flows through the courtyard, (11) .... the visiting children who splash in it. The whole space is designed to be free, accessible and multi-purpose. At night, when the windows of the museum are lit up, the courtyard (12) .... the character of a town square, a place where people can meet friends, eat, drink and relax.

0	A	angle	B	appearance	C	aspect	D	air
1	A	suffer	B	endure	C	uphold	D	bear
2	A	carried	B	supported	C	sustained	D	propped
3	A	blend	B	merge	C	combine	D	mix
4	A	class	B	kind	C	brand	D	set
5	A	reused	B	reclaimed	C	recycled	D	reprocessed
6	A	react	B	behave	C	conduct	D	act
7	A	causes	B	leaves	C	makes	D	creates
8	A	visible	B	evident	C	apparent	D	obvious
9	A	put down	B	cut out	C	cut down	D	put out
10	A	until	B	however	C	even	D	thus
11	A	diverting	B	enjoying	C	delighting	D	rejoicing
12	A	takes in	B	takes up	C	takes on	D	takes over

Use of English Part 3

For questions 1–10, read the text below. Use the word given in capitals at the end of some of the lines to form a word that fits in the gap in the same line. There is an example at the beginning (0).

Performance Art

Performance Art began in the 1960s in the United States and was

(0) ....orginally........... a term used to describe a live event that often   **ORIGIN**

included poets, (1) ......musicians...... film-makers and so on, in   **MUSIC** ✓

(2) ...addition...... to visual artists. predecesors   **ADD** ✓

There were earlier (3) ...precedents.. for this art form, including the   **PRECEDE** ✓

Dadaists in France, who combined poetry and visual arts, and the Bauhaus

in Germany, whose members used live theatre (4) ...workshops... to   **WORK** ✓

explore the (5) ...relationship.. between space, sound and light. By 1970,   **RELATION** ✓

Performance Art was a (6) .....global...... term and its definition had   **GLOBE** ✓

become more specific. Performances had to be live and they had to be art, not

theatre.

Performance Art could not be bought, sold or traded. Performance artists saw

their movement as a means of taking art directly to the public, thus completely

eliminating the need for galleries, agents, (7) ...accountants...and any other   **ACCOUNT** ✓

aspect of (8) ...capitalism... In effect, it became a social commentary on the   **CAPITAL** ✓

need to maintain the absolute (9) .....purity........... of art.   **PURE** ✓

One relatively recent form of Performance Art is 'mobbing', an email-driven

experiment in organising groups of people who suddenly (10) ...materialized   **MATERIAL** ✗

in public places, interact with others according to a very loosely planned scenario,

and then disappear just as suddenly as they appeared.

9/10

A performance artist at work as a human statue

Listening Part 1

(8) **You will hear three different extracts. For questions 1–6, choose the answer (A, B or C) which fits best according to what you hear. There are two questions for each extract.**

You overhear two friends, Maria and David, talking about a book.

1 What do Maria and David agree about?
   A They find the characters in the book very convincing.
   B They immediately found the storyline absorbing.
   C They would like to see the place where the book was set.

2 According to Maria, what is the author's reason for writing the book?
   A to explore a new aspect of human psychology
   B to show that people have different interpretations of the same event
   C to make an interesting point that no one has made before

You overhear two people talking about a piece of jewellery.

3 What does Simon say about the origins of his bracelet?
   A It was chosen as a way to thank him for his hard work.
   B It shows that his uncle had a good opinion of him.
   C It shows he is a man of high rank.

4 What does the bracelet mean to Simon?
   A It helps him understand other people's needs.
   B It provides an easy way to start a conversation.
   C It reminds him that it's important to have clear goals.

You overhear a young woman and her sister talking about clothes for a special occasion.

5 Lauren and her sister both agree that
   A the dress Lauren tries on is a rather unflattering colour.
   B trouser suits always look like office wear.
   C pashminas are a very adaptable clothing accessory.

6 What do we learn about Jack's attitude to clothes?
   A He is not worried about his appearance.
   B He rarely buys expensive clothes.
   C He disapproves of designer clothing.

Leisure and entertainment

Grammar
Ways of linking ideas

❶ Read this article from a magazine and then complete the gaps, using one of the words or phrases from the box below.

what/what	when	whose	how	yet	unless	if
given that	provided	laid out	accepting	arriving		
fascinating	in which	~~that is~~	in ways that	therefore		

MAKING THE MOST OF MUSEUMS

Nowadays there is an increasing emphasis on the idea of life-long education, (1) ....*that is*........... to say, education that continues through the whole of adulthood. One way (2) .... adults can develop their interest in a new subject is to watch television programmes, or read books. A potentially much richer way is to wander through a learning environment, such as a science museum, (3) .... in a systematic way to introduce visitors to particular subjects. With the help of audio-visual aids, computer-assisted instruction and other devices, a museum can bring a subject alive (4) .... compare favourably with a television programme, or a book. The kind of help that museums can give to adults can equally well be given to children, and to teachers (5) .... pupils have come to the museum for specific purposes. At a time (6) .... the demand for public accountability has never been greater, it is worth remembering that many museums receive substantial grants towards (7) .... is supposed to be stimulating educational provision for the general public. Museums (8) .... these grants, (9) .... offering little

more than the occasional public lecture, or very minimal help to schoolteachers (10) .... at the museum with their pupils, (11) .... risk having such financial support severely cut back, or even withdrawn.

Why is this done? The idea is that museums should not simply be aiming to be popular and entertaining, they should also be truly rewarding learning environments. (12) .... this is their aim, they should not just dispense facts and theories. They should show the visitor exactly (13) ....to do with the information (14) .... Isolated snippets of information, (15) .... as they may be, do not encourage museum visitors to use their intelligence. For example, (16) .... told that some fleas can jump 130 times their own height, visitors simply have no idea of (17) .... to apply this knowledge (18) .... they are clearly pointed in the right direction.

❷ Complete the sentences with the most suitable form of the participle (present, past or present perfect), using the verbs in brackets. In some sentences, there may be two possible correct answers.

1 ....Looking...... (look) round the concert hall, I was surprised to see several people I knew in the audience.

2 .... (decide) not to go and play tennis, the two friends went out for a meal.

3 .... (build) 2000 years ago, the Roman amphitheatre is still magnificent.

4 .... (know) by everyone as an outstanding speaker, it was no surprise when my uncle was chosen to deliver a public lecture.

5 'Underfunding is the reason for the youth employment scheme .... (reach) crisis point over the last few weeks,' said the treasurer at the annual meeting.

6 .... (view) through a telescope, the tall ship looked absolutely magnificent.

7 .... (not care) about who might overhear her, Caroline said exactly what she thought.

8 .... (stare) hard at the horizon, I could just make out the tallest of the mountains.

9 .... (write) fifty years ago, the novel addresses issues still of relevance today.

10 .... (find) that he had run out of money, Peter realised there was no point in staying in town any longer.

11 Modern scientific technology .... (produce) safer medicines, few people suffer side effects from them.

12 .... (not understand) what the instructor was saying, one student put his hand up to ask a question.

Vocabulary
The verb *to pay*

❶ ⓐ Complete the sentences, using the prepositions from the box below.

in	for	~~back~~	by	into	to

1 If you lend me £10, I'll pay you ....back........ tomorrow.

2 I'll have to pay a plumber .... fix the problem with the water tank.

3 I'll pay .... the theatre tickets if you'll collect them from the box office.

4 You always pay a bus driver .... cash.

5 I'll go into the bank tomorrow and pay these cheques .... my account.

6 Would you prefer to pay .... cash, cheque or credit card?

ⓑ Match the two halves of the sentence.

1 Installing double glazing pays for itself
2 If you regularly eat too much
3 If you want designer clothes
4 I want to pay my way
5 All that extra training for the race

a is really paying dividends.
b so let's split the bill.
c you'll pay through the nose for them.
d because regular heating bills are reduced.
e you'll pay the price by putting on weight.

ⓒ Which expression with pay means:

1 saves the money it cost – .pay..for..itself.
2 spend too much on something – ....
3 contribute your share of the cost – ....
4 is getting good results – ....
5 experience a bad result from doing something – ....

Writing
A proposal

⊙ **Read this proposal written by a CAE student. Then replace the underlined words, using one of the words or phrases from the box below to improve the vocabulary level.**

such as	compose	taking into consideration
declined	a wide range of	enjoy	personalities
donate	forthcoming events	~~the contents of~~
as well as	had in mind	assistance
professional responsibilities	scheduled	

Sports and Social Club Proposal: publishing a magazine for members

the contents of

This proposal to the committee includes some ideas about (1) ~~what is in~~ the first edition. (2) <u>Thinking about</u> the secretary's suggestions (3) <u>and</u> some ideas from other committee members, I believe that the first edition should contain (4) <u>different</u> subjects to attract the interest of all its readers.

First of all we could include interviews of famous sports (5) <u>people</u> like Gerry Armstrong, the Scottish footballer. I also (6) <u>thought of</u> Joe Hill, the tennis player, but unfortunately he (7) <u>did not accept</u> my invitation due to his (8) <u>job</u>. However, he offered to (9) <u>give</u> his tennis racquets as a prize for our magazine.

Secondly, considering that our readers (10) <u>like</u> keeping fit, I arranged with Ken Brown, the sports centre instructor, to (11) <u>write</u> an article including his ideas and instructions on how our athletes can improve their fitness levels. To make the magazine entertaining, I suggest we should include competitions, (12) <u>like</u> sports crosswords, and also film and book reviews. Also, there should be announcements about (13) <u>what's happening soon</u> at our Club, such as the party and barbecue for our members, which are (14) <u>planned</u> for next month. Finally, I suggest that we should recommend the top restaurants in our town.

I hope that the above suggestions will be of (15) <u>help</u> to the committee for the first edition of our magazine.

Reading Part 4

You are going to read four album reviews from a world music website. For questions 1–15, choose from the reviews A–D. The reviews may be chosen more than once.

In which review is the following mentioned?

the rapid transition from one source of inspiration to another	**1**	
surprise at an artist's lack of success in a venture	**2**	
the artists' obvious enjoyment of the creative process	**3**	
the high standards a performer usually attains in a certain style	**4**	
the varying focus and linguistic origins of the songs	**5**	
negative comment about the words of a song	**6**	
an opening track which impresses without vocals	**7**	
the possibility of diverse reactions to a particular singer	**8**	
the high standards of musicianship maintained throughout the album	**9**	
the problems arising from relying on a multitude of sources	**10**	
a decline in standards after some effective tracks	**11**	
the reliance on certain key musical instruments	**12**	
the calm atmosphere created by two tracks on the same album	**13**	
the special contribution of a singer to a blend of sounds	**14**	
tracks sequenced in a way that would reflect the performers' wishes	**15**	

A Watcha Clan: *Diaspora Hi-Fi – A Mediterranean Caravan*

The album begins with a scrambled montage of voices and Arabic strings and percussion; right away, the listener is projected into a mix of dance floor sounds. This is fusion music, dubbed and electroed. *Watcha Clan* put forward a dilemma: can diverse influences result in a harmonious whole? Or does it just end up as a mish-mash of indistinguishable sound? They certainly add a rich variety of flavours to the dominant rhythms.

Some people can't get enough of vocalist Sista K's unusual voice, but for others even a little is too much. Nassim Kouti sometimes accompanies her on vocals and guitar. One of these tracks is the haunting 'Ch'ilet La'Yani'. The beginning of 'Oued El Chouli' is equally tranquil and briefly entrances before the reggae beat takes over, powered by Moroccan castanets. The song stands out on the album because the really impressive combination of styles works so well. This doesn't always happen on other tracks, but watching the bonus video makes you realise what this band is all about and that they had a lot of fun making this album.

B Various artists: *Nigeria Disco Funk Special*

In the 1970s, Lagos was a creative place musically, and would-be artists flocked there from all over Africa to put their very individual spin on imported music. The first number, an instrumental by *Sahara All Stars* entitled 'Take Your Soul', is bravely funky and strikes just the right opening note. The next outstanding track is by the talented Johnny Haastrup, who gives a great rendition of 'Greetings'. It is hard to understand why he never really made it as a soloist, because this piece is both harmonic and flamboyant.

Sadly, the remaining songs are not in the same league, and you may be disappointed that they lack a truly authentic and traditional feel. Also, the material is mostly instrumental, so there are few singing stars in evidence. But despite this, the album is well worth listening to. It's arranged in an order suitable for clubs, which is doubtless what the artists originally intended.

C Neco Novellas: *Khu Kata*

Neco Novellas is a singer-songwriter with immense talent and imposing stage presence. His new album, 'Khu Kata', presents influences of his teenage years in Mozambique. Guest vocalist Lilian Vieira of *Zuco 103* enriches the track called 'Vermelha' which is a successful mix of Brazilian samba and Mozambican pop, while the track called 'Zula Zula' really shows what Novellas can do. But with 'Phumela' things slide downhill for a while, and the lyrics of 'Swile Navo' can only be described as banal.

He returns to form with 'The Train', which is beautifully arranged and owes an obvious debt to the Hugh Masekela songbook ('Stimela!'), but the best tracks are the uplifting 'Tikona' and 'O Sol', which truly stand out as the blend of world/jazz fusion that this artist regularly delivers. Nonetheless, 'Khu Kata' would have been improved by more rigorous editing and slightly fewer tracks.

D Think of One: *Camping Shaabi*

Think Of One is truly unique. Over the years, this Antwerp-based group have worked and recorded with a wide range of artists such as Afro-Brazilian percussionists and Inuit throat singers, but for this album, they return to Moroccan themes. The Moroccan effect is apparent straight away in the spellbinding rhythms and voices of the first track, 'J'étais Jetée'. And that's just for starters – the recording goes on to mix diverse sounds and types of music at an astounding speed.

The quality doesn't falter from one track to the next and each track is innovative in its own way. The vintage keyboards and Balkan-style brass section are always there, laying the foundations for the other sounds which are brought in and used around them. In a dazzling combination of Flemish, French, Arabic and English, the band's lyrics also fascinate, some having a serious tone and others being more frivolous, but a singable tune always surfaces.

Listening Part 2

(9) You will hear a professional dancer talking to a group of young people about dancing as a career. For questions 1–8, complete the sentences.

To become a [_____ 1] dancer, it is best to start lessons when you are very young.

On degree courses, there is often more emphasis on academic learning than [_____ 2] skills.

In order to make contacts, dance students should attend [_____ 3].

When dancers go to auditions, they should remember to [_____ 4].

Dancers must be prepared to experience [_____ 5] during their careers and develop other skills.

Some dancers refuse to consider [_____ 6] as a way of earning money.

Dancers should try to avoid [_____ 7] which may shorten a career.

Dancers who are unwilling to [_____ 8] are unlikely to do well.

Grammar
Reported speech

1 a Read the article below and then write what the people actually said to the reporter in the speech balloons which follow.

The rise of commuter television

Rail commuters fed up with shouts of 'I'm on a train', the hum of music players and mobile ringtones now have another challenge – televisions. Many rail travellers are already used to TVs in the carriages but televisions are going to be installed in our local commuter trains for the first time. We got on the 8.18 to Manchester to find out what people thought about this.

James French, 25, said he'd been commuting for the last year and he thought it was a pretty good idea because he could watch it if he wanted. If he didn't want to, he'd read a book but his worst nightmare would be constant sport.

Sophie Morton, 17, who travels to school every day, agreed they were a good thing. She said she would stop listening to music and watch the news instead which meant she would be learning something on her way to school.

But most commuters were not keen on the idea.

Natasha Gordon, 27, is American and she said she'd travelled on lots of trains in the US with TV in them and she'd hated it. She wanted to know why the money was being spent on TV when it could go towards improvements in basic services.

Francesco Vecchi, 42, explained that he had to catch the train to work and he objected to TV being forced on him. He was concerned that he wouldn't be able to do vital reading for his job.

We put these points to **Jason O'Donovan**, spokesperson for the railway company. He said that they would never put TV in every carriage and they were going to trial it first as it might be popular in some trains but not others.

I've been commuting for the last year and I think it's a pretty good idea because I can watch it if I want. If I don't want to, I'll read a book but my worst nightmare would be constant sport.

James French

Sophie Morton

Natasha Gordon

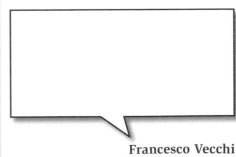

Francesco Vecchi

Jason O'Donovan

ⓑ The reporter asked the commuters the questions below. Use the questions to complete the conversation he had with a colleague.

1 Are you happy about having TV in the train?
2 What do you usually do during your journey?
3 Would you enjoy watching TV on the train?
4 Do you travel on this train every day?
5 How long have you been commuting?

'What did you ask the commuters on the train this morning?'

'I asked them (1) ....*if they were happy*........ about having TV in the train and
(2) .... journey. Most of them seem to read or listen to music. I wanted to know (3) .... watching TV on the train. Most of them didn't think so. I asked them (4) .... every day and (5) .... Most people use the train every day and some have been commuting for years.'

❷ Read what these people said and then complete the reported sentences, using a verb from the box below.

advise ~~announce~~ complain deny doubt enquire urge warn

1 'There will be an extra public holiday next month.'
The President *announced (that) there would be an extra public holiday the following month.*
2 'I don't think Ruth is telling the truth.'
Jamie ....
3 'Are there any job vacancies in the company?'
The man ....
4 'We're being given far too much work.'
The students ....
5 'Don't eat a large meal before going for a run.'
The fitness instructor .... his trainees ....
6 'I didn't tell Frankie the news.'
Joe ....
7 'If I were you, I'd ring Laurie before you turn up.'
Rachel .... them ....
8 'Recycle as much paper as you can.'
The company .... its employees ....

Vocabulary
Television, newspapers and computers

Read the definitions from the *Cambridge Advanced Learner Dictionary* which follow and then complete the gaps by adding the vowels to the correct word from the box below.

BLLTN PSD CNTSTNT TBLD ~~CRCLTN~~ HDLN
BLGGR PDCST KYWRD CMMRCL

1 ......*circulation*......... the number of people to whom a newspaper or magazine is regularly sold

2 .... a significant word used to find out more information about something

3 .... short news programme often about something that has just happened

4 .... a pre-recorded audio programme that's posted to a website and made available for download

5 .... a type of popular newspaper with small pages which has many pictures

6 .... an advertisement broadcast on television or radio

7 .... someone who produces an ongoing narrative, similar to a diary

8 .... a line of words printed in large letters as the title of a story in a newspaper

9 .... someone who competes, often in a quiz

10 .... one of the single parts into which a story is divided when it is broadcast weekly or daily on the television or radio

Writing

Giving a positive or negative impression

1 a ☉ Here are some expressions a CAE student used in a film review. Mark each one according to whether you think they are most likely to be positive (☺) or negative (☹).

A are simply stunning ....☺...............

B really bothered me ....

C the lack of ....

D simply do not move me ....

E manages very ably to ....

F is nothing but ....

G was really impressed ....

H has pleasantly surprised me ....

b ☉ Read the film review written by a CAE student and then complete the gaps, using the expressions A–H from exercise 1a.

I am not a professional critic, but here is my review of the best and worst films I have seen: the best film I have ever watched is most likely *Alien*. Special effects without an interesting story **(1)** ....simply do not move me........ and I usually avoid Hollywood blockbusters but *Alien* **(2)** .... It is a science fiction thriller movie that combines two of my most favourite film genres. The director **(3)** .... create an atmosphere of fear, while teaching us a valuable lesson about the beast we all hide inside. The actors' performances are excellent, especially that of Sigourney Weaver, who is the leading actress. The costumes are well designed and the special effects **(4)** .... The worst film I have ever watched is *200 Warriors*. This film **(5)** .... a combination of impressive special effects with a flat story. Initially I **(6)** .... by the colourful explosions and the epic battles between the good and evil immortal warriors but too many events take place and too few explanations are given. What **(7)** .... is that there is not a single character to identify with and **(8)** .... a strong storyline is a major fault. There is not even a valuable lesson to learn.

Use of English Part 2

For questions 1–15, read the text below and think of the word which best fits each gap. Use only ONE word in each gap. There is an example at the beginning (0).

Effects of television on childhood literacy

Television occupies a large portion **(0)** ......*of*........ children's time. Starting in preschool, children spend more time watching television **(1)** .... participating in any other activity **(2)** .... sleeping. Children also have extensive experience of television before **(3)** .... exposed to many socialising agents, **(4)** .... as schools and peers. Because television has this important role, it is important to understand its potential positive and negative effects **(5)** .... most children.

The results of recent research suggest that there is considerable overlap **(6)** .... the comprehension processes that take place while reading and the processes activated **(7)** .... a period of television viewing. If **(8)** .... , it may very well **(9)** .... the case that children who learn comprehension skills from television viewing before they are ready to read are equipped **(10)** .... some very important tools when they later learn to read.

Clearly, television viewing is not the sole context providing important foundations for literacy. **(11)** .... that most parents are positive about the value of stories, many children may be read **(12)** .... at bedtime. Television, however, is an ideal medium in **(13)** .... to cultivate some of the skills and knowledge needed for later reading. Television is also a visual medium, and thus presents information more concretely than written and spoken text. This content difference across media seems to account **(14)** .... the fact that preschool children are frequently better **(15)** .... recalling televised stories they have watched compared to those they have simply heard.

Use of English Part 5

For questions 1–8, complete the second sentence so that it has a similar meaning to the first sentence, using the word given. Do not change the word given. You must use between three and six words, including the word given. Here is an example (0).

0 There needs to be tighter control than there is at present over what happens in reality TV programmes.

TIGHTLY

Reality TV programmes should be ......*more tightly controlled*...... than they are at present.

1 News programmes should not be allowed to show disturbing images in the early evening.

PREVENTED

News programmes should .... disturbing images in the early evening.

2 I eventually managed to persuade Louisa that I was telling the truth.

SUCCEEDED

I eventually .... Louisa that I was telling the truth.

3 George felt a sense of pride in the achievements of the family business.

PROUD

George .... the family business had achieved.

4 Unless the director gets the actor he wants for the main part, the film will be cancelled.

MEAN

If the director doesn't get the actor he wants for the main part,
it .... the film.

5 The reliability of the Internet as a source of information is sometimes difficult to determine.

HOW

It is sometimes difficult to know .... as a source of information.

6 I only realised that I'd forgotten my wallet when I got to the station.

ARRIVED

It wasn't .... the station that I realised I'd forgotten my wallet.

7 The employees suggested some improvements to the computer system which would make it easier to use.

FORWARD

The employees .... improving the computer system to make it easier to use.

8 Driving without a seatbelt is illegal in most European countries.

AGAINST

It is .... without a seatbelt in most European countries.

Listening Part 4

(10) You will hear five short extracts in which people are talking about their jobs in television.

TASK ONE

For questions **1–5**, choose from the list **(A–H)** each speaker's job.

TASK TWO

For questions **6–10**, choose from the list **(A–H)** what each speaker says they find difficult about their job.

While you listen you must complete both tasks.

A make-up artist

B producer

C actor

D researcher

E sports presenter

F lighting engineer

G sound technician

H costume designer

Speaker 1 [ ] **1**

Speaker 2 [ ] **2**

Speaker 3 [ ] **3**

Speaker 4 [ ] **4**

Speaker 5 [ ] **5**

A having to upset people

B incorporating last-minute changes

C not getting enough variety

D listening to people's problems

E being told what to do

F keeping up to date

G not getting recognition

H working in uncomfortable conditions

Speaker 1 [ ] **6**

Speaker 2 [ ] **7**

Speaker 3 [ ] **8**

Speaker 4 [ ] **9**

Speaker 5 [ ] **10**

Grammar
Tenses in time clauses and time adverbials

❶ ⓐ Read the article below and then choose the correct word or phrase.

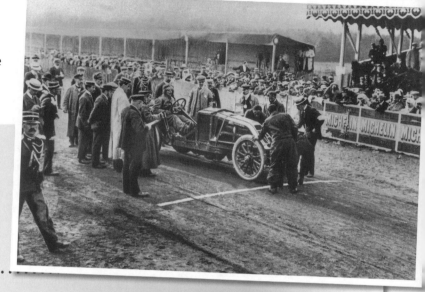

THE HISTORY of GRAND PRIX RACING

Grand Prix racing has its roots in organised automobile racing that began in France (1) *as far back as*/*as long as* 1894. Organisers were keen to exploit motor racing as a showcase for their cars, and the first race, which took place (2) *in*/*on* July 22 of that year, organised by a Paris newspaper, (3) *was held*/*had been held* over the 128 km distance between Paris and Rouen. On that occasion, although Jules de Dion won the race, he (4) *was not given*/*had not been given* the prize because his car (5) *has relied*/*relied* on a mechanical stoker, a device for putting coal into a boiler.

(6) *During*/*Meanwhile,* in 1900, James Gordon Bennett Jnr established the Gordon Bennett Cup in the USA, hoping that the creation of such an international event would encourage manufacturers to improve their cars. However, it was (7) *only when*/*not until* 1906 that the Automobile Club de France organised a Grand Prix on a circuit in Le Mans. The race (8) *was won*/*had been won* by the Hungarian-born Ferenc Szisz in a Renault.

In this (9) *period*/*time*, races were heavily nationalistic affairs, with a few countries setting up races of their own, but no formal championship holding them together. The cars all had a mechanic on board as well as a driver, and these two (10) *allowed*/*were allowed* to work on the cars (11) *during*/*over* the race. Races (12) *were run*/*were being run* over a lengthy circuit of closed public roads, rather than purpose-built tracks, and given the state of the roads (13) *at*/*by* this time, repairs were a common occurrence. Grand Prix races gradually spread through Europe and the US, and in 1924, the many national motor clubs banded together to form an association (AIACR) which was empowered to regulate Grand Prix and other forms of international racing.

Eventually Grand Prix racing (14) *evolved*/*was evolving* into formula racing, and the Formula One so popular now can be seen as its direct descendant. (15) *In*/*To* this day, each event in the Formula One World Championships is still called a Grand Prix.

b Match the two halves of the sentence.

1 I'll cook dinner tonight
2 As soon as I've finished my project
3 I read most of my novel
4 When I know the answer
5 I'll give David his birthday card
6 I'll come straight home
7 When I'd found enough information,
8 When I'd wrapped the present,
9 I injured my wrist
10 I'll get some new strings for my guitar

a while I was sitting on the train.
b while you go to your Spanish lesson.
c I took it straight to the post office.
d I'll hand it in.
e I sat down to complete my project.
f while I was serving for the set.
g while I'm shopping in town.
h when the match is over.
i I'll tell you what it is.
j as soon as I see him tonight.

2 The time expressions in the box below are all used with *at*, *in* or *on*. Write them into the correct circle.

the spring   2010   January   breakfast   the morning
several occasions   the weekend   night   the beginning
dusk   Friday night   six o'clock   midnight   December 12th

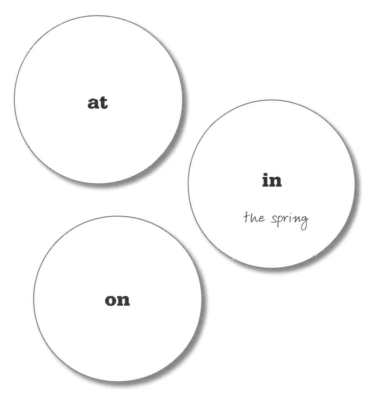

at

in
the spring

on

Vocabulary
Word building

1 a Make the nouns formed from these verbs.

communicate *communication*   compose
discover   evolve
inform   operate
observe   perform
prioritise   proceed

b Complete the table below.

VERB	NOUN	ADJECTIVE	ADVERB
add			
		electrical	
extend			
know			
		medical	
		original	

Writing
Punctuation

Punctuation is very important to meaning and understanding.

Punctuate the paragraph below correctly, using capital letters (A, B, C …), commas (,), full stops (.), apostrophes ('), semi-colons (;) and dashes (–). The paragraph tells you something about the life of John Paul Stapp, who you will read about on pages 48 and 49.

D
dr john paul stapp was born on july 11 1910 in bahia brazil his preliminary education was obtained at the brownwood high school brownwood texas and san marcos academy san marcos texas dr stapp received his first degree in 1931 from baylor university his doctorate from the university of texas in 1940 and his medical degree from the university of minnesota in 1944 he interned for one year at st. marys hospital before entering the us air force in 1944 in 1946 dr stapp was transferred to the aero medical laboratory as a project officer but the job assignment that was the start of his fame came in march 1947 when he was sent to the deceleration project

You are going to read an article about the life of John Paul Stapp. For questions 1–7, choose the answer (A, B, C or D) which you think fits best according to the text.

JOHN PAUL STAPP: THE FASTEST MAN ON EARTH

Captain John Paul Stapp, already a medical doctor, began his scientific career in the 1940s studying the negative effects of high altitude flight, issues absolutely critical to the future of aviation. How could men survive these conditions? The problem of the bends, the deadly formation of bubbles in the bloodstream, proved the toughest, but after 65 hours in the air, Stapp found an answer. If a pilot breathed pure oxygen for thirty minutes prior to take-off, symptoms could be avoided entirely. This

line 10   was an enormous breakthrough. The sky now truly was the limit. The discovery pushed Stapp to the forefront of the Aero Med Lab and he abandoned his plans to become a pediatrician, instead deciding to dedicate his life to research. The Lab's mandate, to study medical and safety issues in aviation, was a perfect match for his talents. It was the premiere facility in the world for the new science of biomechanics.

Stapp was assigned the Lab's most important research project: human deceleration. This was the study of the human body's ability to withstand G forces, the force of gravity, when bailing out of an aircraft. In April 1947, Stapp traveled to Los Angeles to view the 'human decelerator', a rocket sled designed to run along a special track and then come to a halt with the aid of 45 sets of normal hydraulic brakes, which slowed it from 150 miles per hour to half of that speed in one fifth of a second. When it did, G forces would be produced equivalent to those experienced in an airplane crash. The sled was called the "Gee Whiz." Built out of welded tubes, it was designed to withstand 100 Gs of force, way beyond the 18 Gs that accepted theory of the time thought survivable. Early tests were conducted using a dummy called Oscar Eightball, but Stapp soon insisted that conditions were right to use himself as a human guinea pig.

Exercising a modicum of caution on the first ride in December 1947, Stapp used only one rocket. The Gee Whiz barely reached 90 miles an hour, and the deceleration was only about 10 Gs. So Stapp began to increase the number

of rockets, and by August 1948, he had completed sixteen runs, surviving not just 18 Gs but a bone-jarring 35 Gs. Beaten, bruised and battered though he was by the tests, Stapp was reluctant to allow anyone else to ride the Gee Whiz. He feared that if certain people, especially test pilots, were used, their hot-headedness might produce a disaster. Volunteers made some runs, but whenever a new approach was developed, Stapp was his own one and only choice as test subject. There was one obvious benefit: Stapp could write extremely accurate physiological and psychological reports concerning the effects of his experiments.

Yet while the Gee Whiz allowed Stapp to answer the existing deceleration questions, new ones emerged. What could be done to help pilots ejecting from supersonic aircraft to survive? Stapp set out to find the answer on a new sled called Sonic Wind No. 1, which could travel at upwards of 750 miles per hour, and withstand an astonishing 150 Gs. In January 1954, Stapp embarked on a series of runs leading to his 29th and final ride, which took him to above the speed of sound, protected only by a

1　What does the writer mean when he says 'The sky now truly was the limit' (lines 10–11)?
　　A　Stapp had set an unassailable scientific record.
　　B　All previous restrictions on flight had been removed.
　　C　Pilots could now be trained to fly at greater altitude.
　　D　A new design was needed for high-altitude planes.

2　What assessment of Stapp's skills does the writer make in the first paragraph?
　　A　His scientific skills were superior to those of his contemporaries.
　　B　He was able to solve scientific problems at great speed.
　　C　He was able to prove a theory set out by others.
　　D　He was ideally qualified for employment at Aero Med Lab.

3　What was surprising about the construction of Gee Whiz?
　　A　It incorporated a revolutionary new kind of brakes.
　　B　It was initially designed to function without a passenger.
　　C　It could withstand exceptionally high G forces.
　　D　It was not built of conventional materials.

4　Why did Stapp usually insist on doing test runs on Gee Whiz himself?
　　A　He felt his powers of observation were superior to those of other people.
　　B　He was aware that some people were psychologically unsuited to the tests.
　　C　He had little faith in the overall safety of the equipment.
　　D　He thought it was unethical to recruit people for a dangerous task.

5　What was the significance of the experiments on Sonic Wind No. 1?
　　A　They broke all previous speed records.
　　B　They gradually improved deceleration times.
　　C　They set new limits to human potential.
　　D　They proved that people could survive high speeds.

6　How did Stapp respond to becoming a celebrity?
　　A　He avoided appearing in public if he could.
　　B　He was embarrassed by the extent of his fame.
　　C　He responded gracefully to the demands of fame.
　　D　He made use of his fame to achieve a goal.

7　In this text, the writer implies that Stapp's main motivation was
　　A　a desire to minimise loss of life.
　　B　a spirit of adventure.
　　C　a quest for knowledge.
　　D　a wish to be remembered after his death.

helmet and visor. And when the sled stopped, which it did in a mere 1.4 seconds, Stapp was subjected to more Gs than anyone had ever willingly endured. He wasn't just out to prove that people could survive a high speed ejection, he was trying to find the actual limit of human survivability to G force. As Stapp's friend, pilot Joe Kittinger put it: 'It was a point of departure – a new biological limit he was going to be establishing on that run.'

Stapp's life was never the same after that successful run on 10 December 1954. Dubbed 'The Fastest Man on Earth' by the media, his celebrity rose to dazzling heights. Stapp graced the pages of magazines, and became the subject of a Hollywood movie. If the attention was a bit much for the soft spoken Lt. Colonel Stapp, it nevertheless provided him with an opportunity he had longed for – to promote the cause of automobile safety.

For even in the earliest days of the Gee Whiz tests, Stapp had realized that his research was just as applicable to cars as it was to airplanes. At every opportunity, Stapp urged the car industry to examine his crash data, and to design their cars with safety in mind. He lobbied hard for the installation of seat belts and improvements such as soft dashboards, collapsing steering wheels, and shock absorbing bumpers. "I'm leading a crusade for the prevention of needless deaths," he told Time magazine in 1955.

Stapp's work in aeronautics and automobiles continued right up until his death in 1999 at age 89. He had received numerous awards and honors. But the best was the knowledge that his work had helped to save many lives, not just in aviation, but on highways around the world.

Listening Part 2

You will hear a talk about an adventure race called the Marathon of the Sands. For questions 1–8, complete the sentences.

Ali describes the race as both the _____ *and* _____ **1** experience of his life.

Ali realised when he watched a TV programme that a lot of _____ **2** entered the race.

Ali then discovered that he would have to spend a minimum of _____ **3** training.

The training had a negative effect on his _____ **4** and studies.

For Ali, running across the dunes was very hard because sand got into his _____ **5** .

During the 82km stage, Ali got bad _____ **6** on his feet.

All competitors have to carry everything they require except _____ *and* _____ **7** .

Ali eventually finished the race with the help of _____ **8** .

Unit 10 A lifelong process

Grammar
Expressing ability, possibility and obligation

❶ Read this extract from a column in a magazine and then complete the gaps, using *can, must, have to, need* or *be able to* in the correct form – present, perfect or past. Make the verbs negative where you see (*not*) in brackets.

I met someone famous

When I was 13, my school arranged an exchange visit with a school in Canada and a girl called Carrie came to stay with us. She lived in a very isolated area in Canada and she was really excited when she saw that a band was going to play in our town hall.

'This **(1)** ...... *could* ...... be my only opportunity this year to see a live band because at home we **(2)** .... drive a hundred miles to the nearest big city so we don't go very often. But you **(3)** .... (*not*) come if you don't want to', she said to me.

I was happy to go but I knew my parents wouldn't agree. Luckily, my older brother said he would come so I **(4)** .... (*not*) persuade my parents to let Carrie and I go on our own. He **(5)** .... be at work when the tickets went on sale but it was the school holidays so I **(6)** .... queue outside the hall. I got there before the box office opened but I **(7)** .... (*not*) hurried because there was hardly anyone else there and I **(8)** .... get really good seats. I had no idea if the band would be any good and I warned Carrie 'You **(9)** .... (*not*) be disappointed because we don't normally get good bands here so they **(10)** .... be really bad.' She said she didn't mind.

The night arrived and the band started playing. As soon as they went on stage, my brother realised that he knew one of them and when they finished we **(11)** .... go backstage and meet them. It was a really good night and in fact the band actually became famous. We have souvenir programmes which we **(12)** .... sell for a lot of money if we wanted to.

❷ ⊙ Look at these sentences written by CAE students, all of which contain mistakes in the use of modal verbs. Find the mistake in each one and then correct it.

1 The bus got so hot that I felt I ~~can't~~ *couldn't* breathe any more.

2 If you live too far away, you are able to stay at the college's hostel.

3 We don't have to forget how hard women fought to get the vote.

4 I am very sorry but I really couldn't be at the airport when you arrive.

5 When we arrived at the college, we must find our own accommodation.

6 We couldn't wait to see you next week when you come to visit us.

7 I'm determined to work for the company for as long as I'll be able.

8 A lot of my friends have taken their driving test but only a few can pass it on the first attempt.

9 The student study centre isn't as good as it has to be, given the cost of the fees.

10 They wouldn't afford to buy new clothes except on rare occasions.

Vocabulary

Expressions with prepositions: *at, in* and *on*

❶ ⊙ Look at these sentences written by CAE students, each of which contains an expression with a preposition. Choose the correct preposition.

1 You'll find all the information you need *at/in/*(on) the website.

2 You'll be landing *at/in/on* Gerona airport and from there you can get a bus or train to Barcelona.

3 *At/In/On* the last day of my course, we went on a trip together to the seaside.

4 We all have a mobile phone in our family and yesterday they were all ringing *at/in/on* the same time.

5 There was a transport strike so we stayed *at/in/on* the same town for five days.

6 You should wait *at/in/on* the queue until the cashier's light comes on.

7 It's better to sit *at/in/on* the left-hand side of the bus because it's cooler.

8 The train stops *at/in/on* Empoli so you should get off there and change trains.

9 The event is to be held *at/in/on* the first week of July.

10 Please contact me *at/in/on* 76598409932 when my computer is repaired.

11 The bus stop is *at/in/on* the opposite side of the road to my house.

12 I'm a student *at/in/on* a language school in Bristol.

13 At the musical, we sat *at/in/on* the back row and we could hardly see the stage.

14 There's been a huge improvement in the quality of food *at/in/on* the canteen.

15 It was so difficult to choose between the three best entries, so *at/in/on* the end the judges gave three first prizes.

16 You can swim in the sea here *at/in/on* any time of year.

Word building

❷ Read this short article about 'alternative schools' and then put the words in brackets into the correct form.

A different kind of education

While most children attend a mainstream school, there is a tradition in many countries throughout the world of 'alternative schools'. In these schools there tends to be more emphasis on **(1)** .....*creativity*........ (creative) with a greater amount of time spent on the **(2)** .... (participate) of children in artistic subjects and on encouraging pupils' inherent **(3)** .... (fascinate) in the world around them. Mainstream schools do not have the same **(4)** .... (possible) as they tend to be bigger and often have a strict curriculum to adhere to. They do sometimes offer **(5)** .... (provide) for pupils with special **(6)** .... (education) needs, whether that might be extra lessons or help within classes. But for the most part **(7)** .... (conform) is expected amongst pupils. Alternative schools tend to discourage this and praise **(8)** .... (original) in their pupils, giving them the opportunity to express themselves in their own way. This can, of course, be **(9)** .... (disaster) especially if **(10)** .... (attend) at classes is not **(11)** .... (oblige). Most alternative schools require a financial **(12)** .... (contribute) from the parents.

Writing
Ways of linking ideas

Read this student's letter which makes suggestions for ways money could be spent to improve their school. Complete the gaps, using the expressions from the box below.

> In addition,   ~~Outlined below~~   Once again,
> The second point I would like to make is about
>   Another important issue to take into consideration
> The above recommendations   To begin with,   As for
>   It is therefore essential that   Consequently,
> Lastly, I should mention that   There is also

Dear Mr. Newton,

I'm writing on behalf of the students of Saint Paul's College, to express our gratitude for your most generous donation to our committee. **(1)** *Outlined below* are some suggestions for improvements.

(2) .... the library building is very old and in need of complete renovation. **(3)** .... it contains very old chairs and desks and most of them are dirty. **(4)** .... it is not really suitable for studying in. **(5)** .... the variety of books, students are always complaining they can't find what they need. **(6)** .... dissatisfaction with the early closure. Perhaps if we hired extra staff, we would be able to expand the opening hours.

(7) .... the lack of a fully equipped computer centre, which is shameful for a modern school. Today's jobs demand computer skills. **(8)** .... up-to-date computers are purchased immediately.

(9) .... is our sports facilities. It would be marvellous if we could build a sports hall, or even indoor tennis courts and maybe a swimming pool. **(10)** .... the café cannot be used for special events, as it is small and tastelessly decorated.

(11) .... aim to present students' suggestions for necessary improvements. I hope they will prove to be of assistance when it comes to your decisions. **(12)** .... my fellow students and I thank you for your amazing offer.

We look forward to hearing from you.

Yours sincerely,

Cristina Stamouli

Use of English Part 4

For questions 1–5, think of one word only which can be used appropriately in all three sentences. Here is an example (0).

0 Educational reforms will be at the ....*top*........ of the government's agenda next week.
As he left for work, Peter gave his young daughter a quick kiss on the ....*top*........ of her head.
At 4.00 am, the climbers could just see the sun rising over the ....*top*........ of the mountain to the east.

1 The course will .... all the skills I will need in the future.
The light was so bright that I had to .... my eyes.
Because there was little traffic, we managed to .... 200 km in an hour and a half.

2 The timetable was completely .... so we had no time to relax.
The .... impact of the rise in oil prices hasn't yet affected consumers.
Jack was the only one who got .... marks in the test.

3 We need to make some changes to the .... in which we educate our children.
We had to walk a long .... to the beach after we'd parked the car.
I recognised Paul immediately as he has an unusual .... of walking.

4 The students felt they would .... more efficiently if they had their own computers.
I can't get my new camera to .... properly.
Could you .... out how much I owe you?

5 We couldn't decide where to go but we finally .... on Alexandria as the best place.
Payment of your account is now overdue and it should be .... immediately.
Has your son .... in his new school?

Use of English Part 2

For questions 1–15, read the text below and think of the word which best fits each gap. Use only ONE word in each gap. There is an example at the beginning (0).

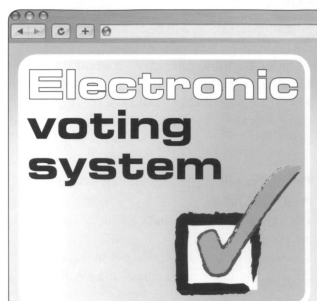

Electronic voting system

Because university lectures (0)..........*are*.............. usually attended (1) .... large numbers of students, there is little interaction (2) .... the lecturer and the students and (3) .... way for the lecturer to check whether the students are benefiting. Thanks (4) .... an invention known (5) .... an electronic voting system – or 'clickers' for short – this situation is beginning to change. 'Clickers' are hand-held devices on (6) .... students click the relevant button to answer questions posed by the lecturer. The students' answers are communicated to the lecturer's computer either by infra-red transmitter (7) .... by radio frequency and the results are displayed on the lecturer's projection screen at the front of the hall. Initially lecturers presumed that the advantage of clickers for students would be

that they would make lectures an interactive, (8) .... than a passive, experience. But there have been unforeseen advantages for the lecturers themselves because they are much more in touch with (9) .... each student is getting (10) .... with the subject. There are advantages for the students because if they get an answer wrong, they won't be embarrassed in front of (11) .... peers. But there are other advantages too. Clickers are also getting students talking to (12) .... other. Some lecturers are getting students to talk to their neighbour about (13) .... they put and why. If clickers are used properly, they have huge potential in allowing lecturers to pitch their lectures (14) .... the right level and get feedback on (15) .... This is especially helpful at the beginning of a course.

Listening Part 1

(12) You will hear three different extracts. For questions 1–6, choose the answer (A, B or C) which fits best according to what you hear. There are two questions for each extract.

Extract One

You hear two people talking in a university about studying abroad.

1 What did Fiona find most difficult about studying at the French university?
   A the range of subjects
   B the methods of teaching
   C the attitude of the lecturers

2 What did Fiona decide about her life as a student at home?
   A She would make more effort to practise her French.
   B She would spend more time with the friends she'd missed.
   C She would try to make friends with foreign students.

Extract Two

You hear two people talking in a shop.

3 What surprised the woman about the products on sale?
   A They cost so much.
   B They seemed very stylish.
   C They were made from recycled materials.

4 What do the speakers agree on about the shop?
   A It has something different to offer.
   B It has copied other similar shops.
   C It will be successful.

Extract Three

You hear part of an interview with a woman who is a trapeze artist in a circus.

5 What does Josie find most satisfying about her job?
   A being able to express herself artistically
   B getting a good reaction from the audience
   C experimenting with new movements

6 She compares herself to a pilot because she thinks they both need to
   A be adaptable.
   B rely on other people.
   C stay calm.

Unit 11 Being somewhere else

Grammar
Conditionals

❶ ⓐ Match the clause on the left to one or more clauses on the right. Find as many correct answers as possible.

1 If you were to find a good guidebook in town
   c, e, g, l
2 If it hadn't been for the terrible weather
3 If you would book the flights
4 If he hadn't been taking so many risks
5 If she's still refusing to speak about it
6 If you could arrive early tomorrow
7 If you don't overheat the coffee
8 If you'll help me with the supermarket shop

a we can be home in half an hour.
b you won't ruin the flavour.
c I'd really appreciate it.
d he wouldn't have fallen off his bike.
e we could look for accommodation.
f we might have really enjoyed the holidays.
g could you buy it for me?
h there's no point in asking any more questions.
i we'll be able to finish it quickly.
j she'd have done some hill-walking.
k he wouldn't be feeling so stupid now.
l do let me know.

ⓑ Complete each of these sentences in two different ways in your own words, using different tenses or modals.

1 I won't be able to travel much unless

   ....

2 I'll bring my sports kit to the gym, otherwise

   ....

3 I'll have to finish this work, or

   ....

ⓒ ⑬ Listen to a short extract from a conversation about holidays and complete the gaps in the dialogue while you listen.

A: ... but we had a fantastic time. So this is one of the pictures I took. The pyramids were absolutely fantastic. Have you ever been there?

B: No, but **(1)** .... ! I'd go like a shot. I didn't have the money when I was a student, but now I'm working,
(2) ....

A: Well, I'd certainly recommend going to Egypt. I'm sure **(3)** ....

B: And **(4)** .... all the well-known sites, just like you did!

A: Well, I certainly loved every minute of my trip. But I didn't realise how hot it would be in August.
(5) .... in April or May instead!

At, in and on to express location

❷ Do you use *at, in* or *on* with these place words? Write *at, in* or *on* next to them.

......*at*..... the airport
.... the phone
.... the beach
.... prison
.... class
.... school
.... the coast
.... the taxi
.... home
.... television

.... hospital
.... the train
.... Italy
.... the top of the escalator
.... my list
.... the meeting
.... the wall
.... the motorway
.... my friend's wedding

Vocabulary
Phrasal verbs: word order with pronouns

Finish the second sentence in each pair so it means the same as the first.

1 We wrapped the present up and gave it to Anna immediately.
   We gave the present to Anna as soon as we had ...wrapped it up... .

2 I enrolled for the art class as soon as I saw they were running one.
   As soon as I discovered they were running an art class, I signed ....

3 When the committee heard that Peter couldn't get there, they cancelled the meeting.
   When the committee heard that Peter couldn't get to the meeting, they called ....

4 I couldn't face going to the dentist, so I postponed my appointment.
   I couldn't face going to my dentist appointment, so I put ....

5 As soon as I realised the trip was going to be on Saturday, I decided not to go.
   As soon as I realised the trip was going to be on Saturday, I dropped ....

This is a good essay, but there are a few things you can do to improve it.

1 In several places I've underlined where you've used the wrong word or expression, and you need to replace them with one of these words:

   apart, everyone, discover, if, age, journey, what, solution, restrict, whether, share, refuse.

2 I've circled six verbs where you've used the wrong form or tense.

3 Please divide your essay into four paragraphs!

Writing
Correcting your writing

⚙ **Read this essay written by a CAE student and the teacher's notes and then rewrite the essay, making the corrections that the teacher suggests.**

Essay: Is it better to travel alone, or with other people?

In my opinion, travelling, is very exciting, and all people, including me, (like) to travel. It helps them to escape from their normal life and to meet new countries, people and cultures. But that which you have to decide is if you should travel alone, or with friends or family. There are advantages and disadvantages in each case. If you travel alone, you are free to go anywhere you want. There is no one who will deny to follow you to the place you want to go! You do anything you want, as you want. However, if you travel alone, you feel extremely lonely. You haven't got anyone to enjoy the travel with. Except from that, a solo trip is more expensive than one with friends or family, because you have to pay for everything yourself and you can't divide the cost with a friend or brother. In case you travel with your friends, you will enjoy the journey more than if you (were) alone. Humans are social creatures and (to be) with someone else is good for your behaviour and your mind. With friends, the travel will not be boring! You can also borrow money from them if you run out. In fact, there aren't many disadvantages if you travel with friends. The only one is that you might disagree with them about the places you want to visit. This isn't a serious disadvantage, because sooner or later you (have) reach a decision. Finally, you could travel with your parents. If you are a young man or woman, travelling with your parents is the best case. You aren't responsible for anything and you go everywhere your parents go. You (haven't) to pay for anything yourself and your family will look after you. However, if you are above the years of eighteen, you won't want to travel with your parents, because this will guide you, which is something you don't want. You (must) want to decide what to do and this is impossible with your parents around. When you are grown up, you don't need your parents watching over you any more!

Reading Part 4

You are going to read an essay about travel writing. For questions 1–15, choose from the sections A–E. The sections may be chosen more than once.

Which section mentions the following?

how concrete detail may inspire creativity

1	

an experience so overwhelming it left people speechless

2	

the compelling nature of youthful impressions

3	

travel writing being a useful tool for a writer to express his ideas with

4	

the way in which human beings attempt to understand the world around them

5	

the writer's attempts to emulate his respected peers

6	

the elusive quality of a human talent

7	

the writer's sense of identification with another's vision

8	

something that is unlikely to be missed when it does not exist

9	

by its nature travel writing cannot be impersonal

10	

an ability to ignore the harsh realities of a place

11	

the dual motivation behind the writer's exploration of what he sees

12	

how a gifted travel writer may change the perception of his craft

13	

a contrast between two responses to the world

14	

a misinterpretation of the significance of an experience

15	

The Temple of the Sun, Baalbek, Lebanon

TRAVEL WRITING

John Biggin is an American who has been inspired to travel and to write about travel since he was a child. This is an extract from one of his essays.

A Great travel writing is infused with a sense of wonder. A phenomenon that cannot be conclusively defined, it remains best comprehended by its effects. A great narrative of travel is the product of a writer for whom the given subject is but a convenient focus – a chance to draw upon a personal vision that exists before and after any number of its expressions. Unfortunately, a sense of wonder cannot be taught or learnt. Rather it is something like a musical sense – if not quite a matter of absolute pitch, then a disposition, something in the genes as different from judgment as the incidence of brown eyes or blue. When it's there, its presence is indisputable; when it's absent, it's not likely to be grieved over.

B Some years ago, I spent a few days in Beirut – one of them on an excursion to Baalbek to see the great temple of the sun associated with its ancient name, Heliopolis. The trip was made in a minibus full of strangers with a Lebanese driver. When our visit to the gigantic ruins was over, we squeezed back into our seats in a stunned silence that seemed the only appropriate response to such awesome magnificence. This spell lasted for many miles, broken, finally, by the muffled syllables with which each of us tried to describe the indescribable. The last to open her mouth was an American who finally uttered the immortal words: "What I want to know," she said, "is how our tour company finds these places."

C In order for the sense of wonder to express itself, it must, professionally speaking, call upon the spirit of investigation. Whereas wonder is a receptive state which simply widens or contracts in response to stimuli, the spirit of investigation is active, charged with curiosity, avid to know how and why things come to be, how they work, to what they may be compared, how they fit into any scheme that may render them comprehensible. It is a spirit concerned with something that can be translated, first for love and then for as much cold cash as may be extracted from the editors of glossy journals. Functioning at its best, the spirit of investigation relates the observer to the observed and makes the exotic familiar.

D By description, measurement, and statistics, the spirit of investigation allows the writer's sense of wonder to go to work. The writer is thus able to unite subjective thoughts with objective evidence, to connect the poetry with the prose and so nudge travel writing away from its current status as a consumer report into a literary genre. And since all travel writing is, inescapably, a form of autobiography, I'd like to cite a few instances, a few fortunate moments when, indulging my own sense of wonder and driven by the spirit of investigation, I tried to find a balance that would justify my pretensions to a place somewhere in the vicinity of those writers whose chronicles of travel experience I most admire.

E Of all the images that passed before my eyes in mid-childhood, two affected me like summonses. One was a colored illustration on the cover of a geography book of the young Christopher Columbus, the man who discovered the Americas, richly dressed in velvet, gazing westward from a deepwater dock in Genoa. There, I thought, was a boy no older than me who, just like me, had the whole world in his head and still looked forward to another. The second was a painting of what seemed to me a celestial city. Situated at the conjunction of a river and an ocean, it was the scene of dazzling energy as flotillas of ships steamed in and out, railroad trains snaked across lacework bridges, and airplanes with open cockpits soared above steeples and tall smokestacks. I knew at first glance I had seen the city of my dreams. The fact that it would turn out to be New London, Connecticut – industrial New London! – did nothing to diminish that first impression. Whenever I'm in New London, and that is often, I simply paste my old fantasy over its reality and go on my way.

Listening Part 3

14 You will hear part of a radio interview in which a writer called Peter Dell is talking about the Brooklyn Bridge in New York. For questions 1–6, choose the answer (A, B, C or D) which fits best according to what you hear.

1 What always happens to Peter each time he arrives at the bridge?

   A He perceives things more lucidly.
   B He experiences a sense of loss.
   C He is reassured by something he looks at.
   D He feels a keen sense of danger.

2 What does Peter become aware of as he walks across the bridge?

   A how vulnerable people on it are
   B how symbolic the bridge is
   C how intrusive the traffic is
   D how important the river is now

3 What surprised Peter about the construction of the Brooklyn Bridge?

   A It was once the longest bridge in the world.
   B Workmen died while they were working on it.
   C It was built from an innovative kind of stone.
   D The weight of the building was supported by timber.

4 According to Peter, how do most pedestrians today react to the Brooklyn Bridge?

   A They think it compares favourably with the skyscrapers.
   B They believe it is one of the most beautiful locations in New York.
   C They experience the excitement of seeing something unusual.
   D They feel almost as if they are walking on air.

5 What does Peter say about the crimes committed involving the Brooklyn Bridge?

   A Some murders have taken place there.
   B The wires on the bridge were sabotaged.
   C There has been one minor explosion.
   D Some confidence tricks were successful.

6 According to Peter, what special quality does the bridge have today?

   A It is sheltered from the worst of the winter weather.
   B It is possible to experience brief moments of silence there.
   C It makes you feel as though you are never alone.
   D Its height above the river makes you feel superior.

Grammar
Uncountable nouns

1 ⓐ Write the uncountable nouns from the box below into the correct place on the diagram.

accommodation	equipment	luggage	stone
advice	~~fruit~~	money	talent
~~bread~~	gas	oil	tea
charm	glass	paper	toothpaste
~~chocolate~~	information	petrol	washing
cloth	intelligence	progress	powder
education	knowledge	research	wood
electricity	leather	soap	wool
			work

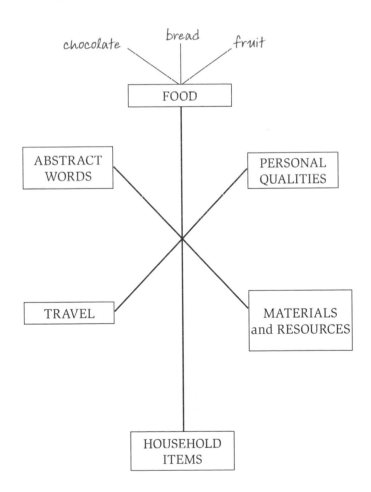

ⓑ Match the two halves of the sentence and then complete the gaps in a–h on the right, using the correct uncountable noun from the diagram in exercise 1a.

1 When I get in from work
2 I tried to start writing my essay
3 The speed of Robert's reply
4 My grandmother claims to dislike flowers
5 There's been a lot in the press
6 Scientists have recently completed
7 Anna kicked the ball straight at the window
8 I pulled into the garage

a and it smashed a pane of ....
b so we took a bowl of .... instead.
c a new piece of .... on bees.
d to purchase a tankful of ....
e I usually make myself a cup of ......tea...... .
f on a clean sheet of ....
g was definitely a sign of his ....
h about the role of ....

Verbs followed by prepositions

2 The verbs in the box below are all followed by a preposition. Write them in the correct column.

~~adapt~~	believe	depend	insist	spend
apply	concentrate	focus	participate	
base	contribute	incorporate	rely	

IN	INTO	ON	TO
			adapt

Articles

❸ Read this extract from a website and then complete the gaps, using the correct form of the article, *a, an, the* or *ø*.

The Global Importance of Coffee

Over **(1)** ....*the*.... last three hundred years coffee has made its way around **(2)** .... world, establishing itself in **(3)** .... economies and lifestyles of **(4)** .... main trading nations. Coffee is now one of **(5)** .... most valuable primary commodities in **(6)** .... world, often second in **(7)** .... value only to **(8)** .... oil as **(9)** .... source of foreign exchange to **(10)** .... developing countries. Millions of people around **(11)** .... world earn their living from **(12)** .... coffee industry.

At times in **(13)** .... history coffee has been hailed as **(14)** .... medicinal cure-all, and at others condemned as **(15)** .... evil brew. In the latter case this was usually for **(16)** .... political or religious reasons, when **(17)** .... coffee houses were at their height of popularity as **(18)** .... meeting places. However, in **(19)** .... last half-century, scientific research has established **(20)** .... facts about coffee, caffeine and our health: in moderation coffee consumption is in no way **(21)** .... health risk, and besides being **(22)** .... most pleasurable experience drinking coffee can indeed confer some health benefits.

Vocabulary
Word building

Complete the table below. Write in the missing abstract noun or verb form. Put an asterisk (*) by the words which have the same form in the verb and noun form.

VERB	NOUN		VERB	NOUN
condemn	*condemnation*		*beautify*	beauty
consume				delight
create				economy
date*	*date*			experience
draw				function
inscribe				industry
portray				popularity
research				practice
survive				supply

Writing
Correcting your spelling

Read this article about Sri Lanka and then add capital letters where necessary and correct any spelling mistakes.

sri lanka is a beautiful island off the southern tip of india, known as the 'pearl of the indian ocean'. i grew up in sri lanka and love to go back as often as i can to see my family. there's a lot to do there, so i always visit the historycal sites, the royal botanick garden and the wildlife sanctuaries.

the conservation of elephants is dear to everyone in my country as they have played such an important role in sri lankan history and culture. they are represented in religios ceremonies, sculture old and new and the arts. the world famous kandy perahera buddhist festival features more than 100 richley decorated elephants in the parade held anually around july/august time.

the last time i was there, i visited the udalawe national park to see elephants in the natural enviroment. the herdes of elephants found in udalawe are the lucky ones because the park is protected and they have plenty of space to roam. unfortunatly not all elephants have this oportunity and this is why conservation projects like this are vital.

i also visited a home for rescued elephants. here they look after orphan elephants; the centre is run by the sri lankan wildlife departement. when elephants are judged ready, they are released into the protected wilderness where rangers monitor their progres to check that they succesfully settle in the park. i stayed at the nearby hotel centauria situated by the chandrika lake. it was an excelent place to stay and offered a good base from which to tour the countryside.

Use of English Part 4

For questions 1–5, think of one word only which can be used appropriately in all three sentences. Here is an example (0).

0   Educational reforms will be at the ....top........ of the government's agenda next week.
As he left for work, Peter gave his young daughter a quick kiss on the ....top........ of her head.
At 4.00 am, the climbers could just see the sun rising over the ....top........ of the mountain to the east.

1   Rice has become an extremely valuable .... commodity in recent years.
The first school young children attend in England is known as a .... school.
The government claimed that its .... concern was to help the less well off.

2   Visitors to the interactive newsroom can .... first-hand what it's like to be a television newscaster.
Stella decided she never wanted to .... the feeling of being totally dependent on someone else.
The force of the wind on the island that night reached a power that no one was ever to .... again.

3   I started to do a lot of overtime work because we .... needed the money to spend on the house.
The teacher told Peter that his essay was very .... set out.
If you leave wooden garden furniture out in the rain, it soon deteriorates ....

4   Many people think it's important to elevate the .... of women in sport.
As a teenager, Paul was very conscious of his .... and wore sunglasses all the time.
In science lessons, pupils still learn how to make a photographic .... using a box with a tiny hole in it.

5   Simon's father never told us exactly what he did for a job, so as children we could only .... the conclusion that he was a spy.
We were not getting anywhere with making a decision, so we decided to .... a line under the discussion.
The psychologist asked his young patient to take a sheet of paper and .... all over it with coloured pens.

For questions 1–12, read the text below and decide which answer (A, B, C or D) best fits each gap. There is an example at the beginning (0).

The Beauty of the Beasts

The earliest known drawings, which survive in the depths of caves in Western Europe, (0) ....C.... back about 30,000 years. The fact that some people (1) .... considerable distances along underground passages in (2) .... darkness to create them is evidence enough that the production of such pictures was an (3) .... of great importance to these artists. But what was their (4) .... ? Perhaps drawing was an essential part of the ceremonials enacted to bring success in hunting. Perhaps the paintings were intended not to (5) .... the death of the creatures portrayed but, (6) .... , to ensure their continued fertility so that the people would have a good supply of meat. We cannot tell. One thing, however, is certain. These drawings are amazingly assured, wonderfully (7) .... and often breathtakingly beautiful.

This practice of painting (8) .... of animals on walls has continued throughout our history. Five thousand years ago, when people in Egypt began to build the world's first cities, they too inscribed animals on their walls. There is no (9) .... about the function of at least some of these: the Egyptians (10) .... animals as gods. But they also (11) .... in the natural beauty of the animals, adorning the walls of their underground tombs with their pictures, so those in the next world would be (12) .... of the beauties and delights of this one.

0 **A** originate   **B** belong   **C** date   **D** exist

1 **A** approached   **B** crawled   **C** dawdled   **D** proceeded

2 **A** whole   **B** entire   **C** full   **D** complete

3 **A** act   **B** exploit   **C** operation   **D** execution

4 **A** profit   **B** principle   **C** purpose   **D** procedure

5 **A** take over   **B** bring about   **C** put across   **D** make out

6 **A** in contrast   **B** on the contrary   **C** not at all   **D** on the other hand

7 **A** right   **B** correct   **C** accurate   **D** true

8 **A** copies   **B** appearances   **C** reflections   **D** images

9 **A** difficulty   **B** reason   **C** problem   **D** doubt

10 **A** celebrated   **B** praised   **C** worshipped   **D** adored

11 **A** delighted   **B** loved   **C** enjoyed   **D** appreciated

12 **A** reminisced   **B** reminded   **C** recalled   **D** recollected

Listening Part 1

(15) **You will hear three different extracts. For questions 1–6, choose the answer (A, B or C) which fits best according to what you hear. There are two questions for each extract.**

Extract One

You will hear part of a radio discussion about Monarch butterflies.

1 According to the man, in what way do Monarch butterflies differ from other butterflies?

  A They fly very long distances.
  B They spend the winter in a warm climate.
  C They survive best at high altitude.

2 What does the man find surprising about the Monarch butterfly?

  A They can only migrate once.
  B They migrate in large groups.
  C They migrate to an exact location.

Extract Two

You overhear two friends talking about the final of a cookery competition they saw on television.

3 The speakers agree that the winning contestant
  A performed well at a crucial moment.
  B fully deserved to win the contest.
  C used an intriguing range of ingredients.

4 The woman thinks that yesterday's cookery programme could be improved by
  A adding a new person to the judges' panel.
  B varying the format of the presentation.
  C specifying what style of cooking contestants must do.

Extract Three

You will hear two friends discussing a trip to a game park in South Africa.

5 Before Lauren went to South Africa, Peter said that
  A the sheer size of the animals would be impressive.
  B the game park would be the highlight of the trip.
  C the sunsets were spectacular in this kind of landscape.

6 Lauren thought the elephant approached their jeep
  A because it wanted to warn them off.
  B because it was searching for food.
  C because it was simply curious.

Grammar

The language of comparison

❶ **Look at the photographs and then write sentences comparing them, using the comparison words in brackets.**

1 (less) The people rafting are having a less relaxing time.
2 (much) ....
3 (not so) ....
4 (fewer) ....
5 (a great deal) ....
6 (by far) ....

❷ 16 **Read what a student said about the photographs and then complete the gaps, using the conjunctions and adverbs in the box below. You will need to use some of them more than once. Then listen and check your answers.**

| but whereas however even if although despite |

The people in the top picture look as though they're having to work really hard. That's probably because white-water rafting tends to be a very serious hobby **(1)** ......whereas.......... rowing can be enjoyed by anyone. Some people won't agree with that, **(2)** .... , because they'll say you can be very serious about rowing too. I just mean that anyone can go rowing on a lake **(3)** .... they haven't made any preparations **(4)** .... it's more important to plan properly if you go rafting. The weather can change suddenly in the mountains and it doesn't look very good in this picture. They seem to have decided to go rafting **(5)** .... the bad weather **(6)** .... maybe it wasn't like that when they started. These people must have planned their

trip properly as they seem to have the right equipment with them.

(7) .... rafting can be quite dangerous, some people have been known to attempt it without the right equipment. I've only ever been rafting once – we didn't have all the right things and I got really scared. After that, I decided rafting wasn't for me. I wouldn't go again **(8)** .... you paid me!

Vocabulary
Word building

Read this short article about allergies and then put the words in brackets into the correct form.

Allergies: their causes and treatment

The number of people in Britain receiving a new
(1) ......*diagnosis*........ (diagnose) of allergies such as
asthma, eczema and hay fever is increasing by five
per cent every year.
There is some **(2)** .... (evident) to show
that Britain's **(3)** .... (obsess) with rules
and regulations to ensure **(4)** .... (clean)
in the home, supermarket and workplace is reflected
in the number of allergy **(5)** .... (suffer).
One theory is that we have far less
(6) .... (expose) to dirt and germs during
childhood than we used to have, so our bodies do not
have the opportunity to develop a **(7)** ....
(resist) to allergens. While we may look down on the
(8) .... (hygiene) approach to food and
general living which people had in the past, there are
some lessons we could learn today by maybe being a
bit less cautious.

Nobody would dispute the importance of
(9) .... (medicine) advances. These
include vaccinations given routinely to children which
have revolutionized our lives by providing
(10) .... (immune) to some life-
threatening diseases. There is, however, some
controversy over whether they actually
(11) .... (weak) our immune systems and
are being given unnecessarily for diseases which are
not dangerous. In the meantime, a whole industry has
developed around preventative medicines which are
very **(12)** .... (effect) in treating allergies.

Writing
Formal writing

⊙ **Read this report written by a CAE student. First, choose the most suitable formal expression and then write a suitable heading for each of the paragraphs, A–E.**

Report to the Principal about the proposals from the three catering companies

A ....*Introduction*..........
The aim of this report is to **(1)** *give /* *point out* the
advantages and disadvantages of three proposals, which
the college has received. Students have been complaining
about
(2) *not having / the lack of* healthy food, so I have
(3) *examined / looked at* what each proposal offers.

B ....
Kavanagh Catering Services (KCS) **(4)** *talk about offering /
propose to offer* fast food and snacks **(5)** *throughout the
day / all day*, but **(6)** *they don't say / there is no mention
of* how healthy they are. Rainbow Ltd (RL) **(7)** *emphasise /
say* that their meals are all made from fresh ingredients.
Xanadu Express (XE) offer nutritious food and even herbal
teas.

C ....
Students eat at the college five times a week so variety is
(8) *crucial / needed*. KCS offer fast food and snacks and
only some hot meals, but they don't **(9)** *state / say* how
often their menu changes. RL say they offer a wide choice
of hot meals and salads. XE, who say their menu changes
daily, have a choice of two hot dishes a day but **(10)** *it
doesn't look like they / they don't appear to* include any
snacks.

D ....
XE would offer the best opening hours as they
(11) *guarantee / promise* to stay open from 8am to 10pm.
Then comes KCS who would be open from 8am to 8pm,
but they stop serving food in the early evening. RL are only
open from 9am to 6pm, and they only serve hot meals for
a **(12)** *short / limited* time from 12–2.

E ....
I recommend that we **(13)** *accept / agree to* the proposal
from RL even though they only serve hot meals from 12–2.
It is not possible for students to eat a full meal at any
other time, and RL still offer snack food during the
(14) *remainder / rest* of the day. They also promise a
variety of food.

Reading Part 1

You are going to read three extracts which are all concerned in some way with sport. For questions 1–6, choose the answer (A, B, C or D) which you think fits best according to the text.

Coaching athletes for competitions

A recent report highlights the dramatic role a coach plays in the training and reinforcement of an athlete's mental toughness, motivation, commitment, and, ultimately, willpower. Without these vital characteristics the athlete will be unable to produce the required consistent intensity and effort in the training situation and as a result will not attain their true performance level in competition. Rehearsal of strategies in training including the use of simulation training to 'recreate' the key moments of pressure experienced in competition, but in a controlled environment, can be an invaluable approach to preparing the athlete for the very real challenges of competition.

Mike Powell, award-winning sports photojournalist

I've seen some large and excited sports crowds when I've been covering major stadium-based events, but they were nothing compared to forcing my way up a mountain on a motorcycle during the 1995 Tour de France ahead of the competing cyclists. I think if that climb could boast the largest single-day live sports crowd on record, I'd believe it. We had to push our way through them in order to keep moving up, all the time turning round and shooting the action as the cyclists made their way upwards. I finished the day with my face blackened and my mouth tasting of road tar, but it still stands out as an experience of a lifetime.

Covering lots of different sports events has helped one skill to become ingrained in me: timing. Moving away from event coverage and working one-on-one with athletes, dancers and sports models has allowed me to concentrate on the clean lines and form that I always tried to isolate during a game. I break down their motion in my head into multiple frames, and choose one to shoot. Shooting action in the studio is great as you get to boil the whole process down to its minimal form. You can't hide behind a great location or the emotion of the event. I like the simplicity of that. Of course great locations are always fun, but I like to go out when the weather is miserable. It adds an element of struggle to the sport.

1 When the photographer looks back to the day he spent at the 1995 Tour de France, what stands out about it for him?

    A the speed of the race
    B the steepness of the mountain
    C the number of spectators
    D the standard of the cyclists

2 The photographer's main aim when photographing sportspeople is to

    A capture the movements they make.
    B demonstrate the interaction between them.
    C show the impact of a location.
    D convey the atmosphere of an event.

This process is by no means limited to environmental or physical parameters. Developing competence in athletes in mental exercises including imagery can lead to greater self-belief. A recent article highlighting ways in which a coach can encourage athletes to use imagery identifies recent information on imagery use and dispels some of the myths associated with this form of training. Key areas where imagery can be employed are 'strategic imagery' where, for example, a gymnast may visualize their whole routine to increase the natural flow of their performance; 'goal-oriented imagery' based on visualizing the outcome - for example standing on a medal podium; the use of 'imagery for mastery and maintaining control' through rehearsing various scenarios during an event and practicing how to react and deal with that situation through imagery.

3 According to the text, what contribution can a coach make to help an athlete achieve their potential?

   A make sure their efforts in training are recognised
   B prepare them to deal with stressful situations
   C show them how to learn from any failures
   D create a training programme which builds up gradually

4 What is the writer trying to do in the second paragraph?

   A illustrate situations which an athlete might find difficult to deal with
   B explain why a procedure should be used by athletes with care
   C give proof that a training approach has been shown to work
   D suggest ways in which a technique can be put into practice

Extract from a novel: A game of squash

Henry kneels to settle his valuables in a front-wall corner of the squash court. There's a momentum to the everyday, a Saturday morning game of squash with his good friend and
line 5 colleague, that he doesn't have the strength of will to interrupt. He stands on the backhand side of the court and his opponent, Jay, sends a brisk, friendly ball down the centre, automatically Henry returns it, back along its path. And so

they are launched into the familiar routines of a warm-up. The third ball Henry mishits, slapping it loudly into the tin. A couple of strokes later he stops to retie his laces. He can't settle. He feels slow and encumbered and his grip feels misaligned, too open, too closed, he doesn't know. He fiddles with his racket between strokes. Four minutes pass and they've yet to have a decent exchange. There's none of that easy rhythm that usually works them into their game. He notices that Jay is slowing his pace, offering easier angles to keep the ball in play. At last, Henry feels obliged to say he's ready. Since he lost last week's game he is to serve. This is the arrangement they always have.

5 When the writer says Henry 'doesn't have the strength of will to interrupt' (line 5), he is referring to interrupting

   A his good friend.
   B the game of squash.
   C Saturday morning.
   D the momentum.

6 Although he's playing badly, Henry feels obliged to say he's ready because

   A he accepts that he is not going to play well against Jay.
   B he realises that Jay is getting impatient with him.
   C he doesn't want Jay to think he's reluctant to start the match.
   D he knows that Jay will not enjoy being beaten.

Listening Part 2

(17) You will hear a talk about the history of surfing. For questions 1–8, complete the sentences.

HISTORY of SURFING

It is now generally agreed that surfing started about [_____ **1**] ago in Western Polynesia.

The first surfers were [_____ **2**] who used surfing as a way of getting ashore.

In ancient Hawaii, the best surfers came from the [_____ **3**] social class.

The person making a board would leave fish as a [_____ **4**] to the gods of the tree he had dug up.

The type of surfboard used by children was called a [_____ **5**] board.

The 'olo' was a surfboard that only [_____ **6**] could use.

In the 20th century, a swimmer called Duke Kahanamoku made surfing popular in Europe, Australia, [_____ **7**] and the USA.

Modern surfboards vary in and [____ *and* ____ **8**], but all have three fins and are made of fibreglass.

Unit 14 Moving abroad

Grammar
Emphasis: cleft sentences

❶ Read each pair of sentences and then complete the gap in the second sentence.

1 George didn't have anywhere to live over the summer so he rented a caravan by the beach.

   George didn't have anywhere to live over the summer so what .... _he did was rent_ .... a caravan by the beach.

2 The local football team need a good manager to help them achieve their potential.

   All .... to help them achieve their potential.

3 I decided to apply to this college because of the excellent sports facilities.

   It was because of

   .... this college.

4 I want to save enough money to take flying lessons.

   What .... flying lessons.

5 Every morning he checks his emails before he does anything else.
   The first thing
   .... his emails.

6 If your credit card is stolen, you should ring the emergency number immediately.

   What .... the emergency number immediately.

Comment adverbials

❷ Add an adverb from the box below to each sentence. Do not change the form of any of the words.

> admittedly   coincidentally   typically   wisely   ~~wrongly~~
> up to a point

1 The chauffeur was ∧accused [*wrongly*] of giving the newspapers the story when in fact he knew nothing about it.

2 The organisers of the marathon changed the start of the race from 11am to 7am because of the heat in the middle of the day.

3 Ruth named her baby Amber and her cousin in Australia chose the same name for her baby.

4 I agree with you that technology makes our lives easier but it also means we can never properly relax.

5 I got the job because my father is managing director.

6 We were taken to eat in a village restaurant where the food they served was Portuguese rather than an international mix.

Vocabulary

Phrasal verbs with *give*, *do* and *make*

❶ a **Read these groups of sentences and then decide which verb (*give*, *do* or *make*) completes all three gaps in each group.**

1   I never .... up an excuse if I don't want to do something as I prefer to tell the truth.
Miguel offered to take me out for a meal to .... up for forgetting my birthday.
I opened the door but it was so dark I couldn't .... out who was there.

2   Reviewers shouldn't .... away the endings of the films they write about.
They can't bear it when their children cry so they always .... in and buy them what they want.
The old electric fire doesn't .... off much warmth.

3   It costs a fortune to .... up an old house.
I've forgotten to bring my MP3 player but I can .... without it.
I've got a really difficult decision to make and I could .... with some advice.

b **Now match the nine phrasal verbs from exercise 1a to their definitions below. Always try to learn phrasal verbs with their meanings and an example sentence.**

Phrasal verb	Meaning
1	to say something untrue
2	to manage even though you don't have something
3	to repair or decorate
4	to finally agree after refusing
5	to need or want something
6	to provide something good to improve a bad situation
7	to say something that should be kept secret
8	to hear or see something, usually with difficulty
9	to produce light, a smell, heat or a gas

Writing

Checking your writing

❶ ⊙ **Read this information sheet written by a CAE student. First, find and correct eight grammatical errors the student made and then complete the gaps, using one of the adverbs from the box below to add emphasis.**

at least	unfortunately	definitely	literally

INFORMATION SHEET FOR STUDENTS FROM ABROAD!

When you arrive ~~to~~ *in* a new country it is very different and it could be helpful to follow some advice. Here are some important things about how to managing your money while you are studying at the college.

Find a cheap place to stay in first of all. If you don't want to share your space with others, it could be expensive. Having a comfortable place is good but the cost is the most important thing. I think that you should share **(1)** .... the kitchen and bathroom. But I recommend that you try to find a big place with your friends and then you can all contribute in the expenses.

Even if you choose to be alone you should made sure that it is possible to cook your own food. Eat out in a restaurant is enjoyable but **(2)** .... it is expensive as well. Having dinner out every now and again especially with friends makes you appreciating this kind of treat. You can **(3)** .... save money by shopping at a big supermarket once a week, then you can avoid to buy expensive food every day.

Deciding whether to spend money on entertainment or not is difficult. In the city centre there are **(4)** .... hundreds of things to do. Lots of them are, however, very expensive. It is the same with clothes and restaurants. I would suggest you to find other places, a little bit further away where you can easily save money and still have the same fun.

GOOD LUCK!

❷ Find the sentences in exercise 1 on page 72 which can be rewritten to add emphasis and then complete the sentences below.

1 The first thing you have to do is ....
2 Having a comfortable place is good but it's ....
3 Finding a big place with your friends ....
4 Shopping at a big supermarket ....
5 The most difficult thing to decide ....

Use of English Part 2

For questions 1–15, read the text below and think of the word which best fits each gap. Use only ONE word in each gap. There is an example at the beginning (0).

Ellis Island

Ellis Island is a small island in New York Harbour **(0)** .....which..... has played a crucial part in the history of the United States. **(1)** .... 1892 and 1954, over twelve million immigrants entered the United States through Ellis Island, designated as the site of the first Federal Immigration Station by President Benjamin Harrison in 1890. Before this, **(2)** .... to its rich and abundant oyster beds, it **(3)** .... been known as Oyster Island. Annie Moore, a 15 year-old Irish girl accompanied **(4)** .... her two brothers, entered history and a new country as **(5)** .... very first immigrant **(6)** .... be processed at Ellis Island on January 2, 1892. Over the next 62 years, many more immigrants **(7)** .... to follow through this port of entry and go **(8)** .... to make new lives in their adopted country. It has been estimated that nearly half of all Americans in different parts **(9)** .... the United States today can trace their family history to at least one person who passed through the Port of New York at Ellis Island.

From 1984, Ellis Island underwent a major restoration project and the main building was reopened to the public on September 10, 1990 as the Ellis Island Immigration Museum. Nearly a century **(10)** .... the peak years of immigration, it is **(11)** .... of the most popular tourist destinations in the National Park Service and receives almost two million visitors annually, many of **(12)** .... take the opportunity to find **(13)** .... about their ancestors. More **(14)** .... 100 million Americans may find records of **(15)** .... family's arrival there.

Use of English Part 3

For questions 1–10, read the text below. Use the word given in capitals at the end of some of the lines to form a word that fits in the gap in the same line. There is an example at the beginning (0).

Advice to families moving abroad

When a family moves to a new country they need to think about how
they will maintain their own language and **(0)** ...... *encourage* .... their   **COURAGE**
children to learn a new one. Not **(1)** .... the experience   **SURPRISE**
of being dropped into a group of people who do not speak their language
can be **(2)** .... for children – although there is plenty of   **PUZZLE**
(3) .... to show that very young children seem to cope   **EVIDENT**
much more easily than their parents!

In a new country, there are moments when the children need
(4) .... from their parents and when it may   **REASSURE**
be more crucial than ever to maintain routines which are
(5) .... important such as story-telling in the home   **EMOTION**
language. These routines **(6)** .... a shared history and   **SYMBOL**
the permanence of the **(7)** .... between parent and   **RELATION**
child.

It is **(8)** .... not to start speaking the new language   **PREFER**
to your child when at home. The importance to the child of associating
parental relations with one particular language should not be
(9) .... and one can easily imagine how stress at school   **ESTIMATE**
coupled with a sudden switch of language at home may be interpreted by
the child as a kind of **(10)** .... particularly at a moment   **DENY**
of general upheaval for the whole family.

Listening Part 2

You will hear a man called Adam talking to a group of people about living in Romania. For questions 1–8, complete the sentences.

Adam's wife is Romanian and he was recently offered a job as [_____ 1] in Romania.

His wife found a flat but then they had to buy [_____ 2] in a hurry.

Where climate is concerned, he finds the [_____ 3] more difficult to deal with than he expected.

Adam and his wife spend leisure time in the mountains where he enjoys [_____ 4].

Adam says [_____ 5] is not very good in the part of the city where he lives.

Adam disagrees with people who say that [_____ 6] is the best local food.

Because of his poor knowledge of the language, Adam doesn't often go to the [_____ 7].

Adam thinks Romanian people have more [_____ 8] for social events than people in Scotland.

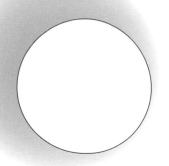

Acknowledgements

Development of this publication has made use of the Cambridge International Corpus (CIC). The CIC is a computerised database of contemporary spoken and written English which currently stands at over one billion words. It includes British English, American English and other varieties of English. It also includes the Cambridge Learner Corpus, developed in Collaboration with Cambridge ESOL Examinations. Cambridge University Press has built up the CIC to provide evidence about language use that helps to produce better language teaching materials.

The authors and publishers acknowledge the following sources of copyright material and are grateful for the permissions granted. While every effort has been made, it has not always been possible to identify the sources of all the material used, or to trace all copyright holders. If any omissions are brought to our notice, we will be happy to include the appropriate acknowledgements on reprinting.

Penguin Books Limited and David Godwin Associates for the adapted text on pp. 8–9 'A Visit Home' from *The Farm* by Richard Benson (Hamish Hamilton, 2005). Copyright © Richard Benson 2005. Reproduced by permission of Penguin Books Limited; Rogers, Coleridge & White for the adapted text on p. 18 'The Cocktail Party Effect' by Claudia Hammond, *Psychologies*, March 2008. Copyright © 2008 Claudia Hammond; *Financial Times* for the adapted text on pp. 18–19 'Book Review: What is Intelligence' by James R Flynn, *Financial Times* 10 November 2007. Copyright © Financial Times Limited, 2007; *Radio Times* magazine for the adapted text on p. 19 'What's in a Face?' *Radio Times*, 3–9 March 2001. Reproduced by permission of *Radio Times* magazine; Lisa Belkin for the adapted text on p. 23 'Putting some fun into the workplace' from 'Life's Work: Putting some fun back into 9 to 5' *New York Times*, 6 March 2008. Reproduced by permission of Lisa Belkin. Telegraph Media Group Limited for the adapted text on pp. 28–29 'The Scariest Ride on the Planet' by Charles Starmer-Smith, *The Daily Telegraph*, 8 February 2008 and for the adapted text on p. 64 'The Beauty and the Beasts' by David Attenborough, *The Daily Telegraph*, 24 February 2007. Copyright © Telegraph Media Group Limited; University of Michigan-School of Education for the adapted text on p. 43 'Effects of television on childhood literacy' from 'The role of television viewing in the development of reading comprehension' by Paul van den Broek, www.ciera.org/library/archive/2001-02/200102pv.pdf; Adapted text on p. 47 from *Autospeed*, 21 April 2008; Nick T. Spark for the adapted text on pp. 48–49 'John Paul Stapp: The Fastest Man on Earth' from www.ejectionsite.com/stapp.htm. Reproduced by kind permission of Nick T. Spark; Adapted text on p. 59 'Travel Writing' from the *Joy of Travel: Vagablogging* by John Brinnin; The British Coffee Association Information Service for the adapted text on p. 62 'The Global Importance of Coffee' from *The History of Coffee, Global Appeal*, 13 May 2008. Reproduced by permission of The British Coffee Association Information Service; CSMA for the adapted text on pp. 62–63 from 'Trunk Call' by Asoka Partridge, *Motoring & Leisure*, February 2008. Reproduced by permission of CSMA; Mike Powell for the text on p. 68 from 'When you learn how to shoot sports in an era of manual focus and slow-motor drives, you learn how to pick your moment' *Sublime Magazine*. Reproduced by permission of Mike Powell, www.mikepowellphoto.com; Brian Mackenzie for the adapted text on pp. 68–69 'Coaching athletes for competitions' from 'Now you can deal with your own stress what about your athlete?'

www.brianmac.co.uk. Reproduced by permission of Brian Mackenzie; Random House Group Limited, Knopf Canada and Rogers, Coleridge & White for the text on p. 69 from *Saturday* by Ian McEwan, published by Jonathan Cape. Reprinted by permission of The Random House Group Limited, Knopf Canada and Rogers, Coleridge & White on behalf of the author; Cambridge University Press for the adapted text on p. 74 'Advice to families moving abroad' from *The Bilingual Family* 1st edition, 1986, by Edith Harding and Philip Riley. Copyright © Cambridge University Press. Reproduced with permission; Guardian News & Media Ltd for the adapted recording on p. 35, Extract Two and the audio recording from 'It's about what we've created together' by Joanna Moorhead, *The Guardian*, 9 February 2008. Copyright Guardian News & Media Limited 2008.

Key: l = Left, r = Right, t = Top, bk = Background, b = Bottom, c = Centre, u = Upper, w = Lower, f = Far

For permission to reproduce photographs: Courtesy of the Air Force Flight Test Center History Office p. 48; Alamy/ (Visions of America, LLC) p.6, / (Christopher Pillitz) p. 18(r), /(Royal Geographical Society) p. 26, / (Jon Arnold Images Ltd) p. 34,/(David Pearson) p. 36, / (Dance by Beytan) p. 40, / (Martin Shields) p. 52, / (ImagesEurope) p. 64; Bubbles Photolibrary p. 10; Bridgeman Art Library p. 16 *Flaming June*, c.1895 (oil on canvas) by Leighton, Frederic (1830–96) Museo de Arte, Ponce, Puerto Rico, West Indies/ © The Maas Gallery, London, UK; Corbis/ (Robert Eric / Sygma) p. 18(l), / (Maher Attar / Sygma) p. 58, / (Bettmann) p. 60, /(JLP/Jose L. Pelaez) p. 74; Lorenzo Fanchi/StageShots.nl p. 39; Getty Images/ (Patti McConville) p. 25(r),/ (Tim Sloan / AFP) p. 33, / (Pierre Verdy / AFP) p. 50, / (Stephen Studd) p. 56, / (VCL/Tim Barnett) p. 66(t), / (Mike Powell) p. 68; Gary Gilbert, Director of Photography/Photo Editor, Boston College Magazine, Office of Marketing Communications p. 54; iStockphoto (Remus Eserblom) p. 75; Lebrecht Music & Arts Library p. 46; Lonely Planet Images p. 62 (Michael Aw); Jane Naughton p. 9; Photolibrary. com p. 20, p. 21(l), p. 25(l); Photoshot / (Blend Images) p. 23, / (Band Photo / uppa.co.uk) p. 55; Punchstock/ (Blue Moon) p. 21(r), / (Pure Stock) p. 65, /(Digital Vision) p. 66(b); Rex Features/ (Jeff Gilbert) p. 29,/ (Photo by Roger-Viollet) p. 73; Ronald Grant Archive p. 45 (©BBC); Superstock (© Ingram Publishing) p. 30; *The Thirteenth Tale*, author Diane Setterfield, Orion Fiction, an imprint of The Orion Publishing Group; London p. 31; www.railimages.co.uk / photographersdirect.com for p. 41.

The publishers are grateful to the following contributors:

Proofreader: Marcus Fletcher
Picture researcher: Kevin Brown

Recordings produced by John Green, TEFL Tapes, edited by Tim Woolf, recorded at id audio, London.

Illustrations: Martina Farrow: p. 11, p. 66; Joy Gosney: p. 37; Mark Blade: p. 62; Mike Renwick p. 70;

Cover design by Wild Apple Design Ltd.

Designed and typeset by Wild Apple Design Ltd.